Inviting Bilingual Writers into the CONVENTIONS OF SPANISH

Grades 1–5

JEFF ANDERSON with **Whitney La Rocca**
Spanish Adaptation by **Caroline Sweet**

Stenhouse Publishers
Portsmouth, New Hampshire

Library of Congress Cataloging-in-Publication Data is on file with the Library of Congress.

ISBN 978-1-62531-332-4

Cover and interior designs by Martha Drury
Typeset by Drawing Board Studios

Manufactured in the United States of America

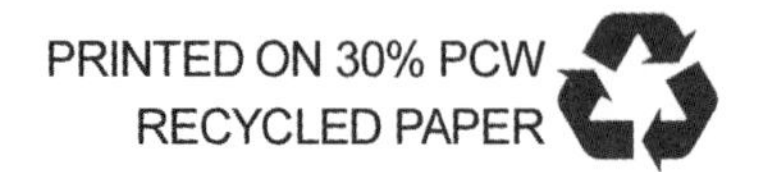

25 24 23 22 21 20 19 9 8 7 6 5 4 3 2 1

To Peggy Sweet, who dedicated thirty-five years to teaching the students who needed her most.

—CS

Contents

Introduction

Porque soy bilingüe
puedo leer libros y books . . .
—*Bilingüe,* Alma Flor Ada

If you're reading this book, you likely had a period of time where you learned either English or Spanish as a second language. You had to pay close attention to the patterns of language. Perhaps you repeated, even chanted, certain patterns over and over. And if you are reading this book, it's likely that you spend your day as an educator working with students who are all in different places in their journeys to bilingualism. You likely have a classroom filled with *libros* and books. And you want those texts to inspire possibilities in your students—to see that they, too, can share their world through writing. But how do we create not just readers but writers in our classrooms? How do we give students the tools to tell their own stories, write their own *libros* and books?

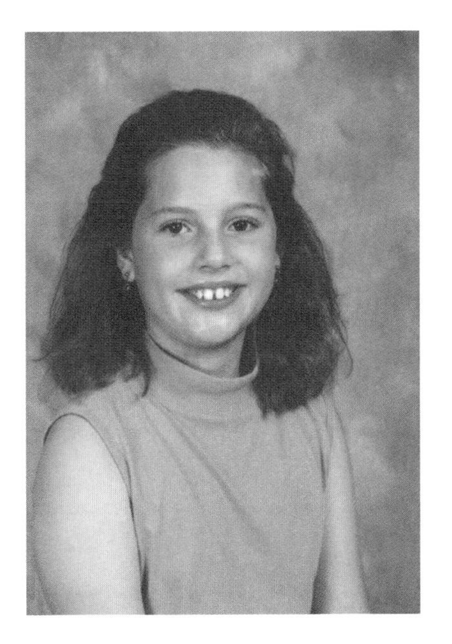

Like many, I found answers to these questions in the original *Patterns of Power*, where Jeff Anderson and his co-writer Whitney La Rocca (2017) introduce teachers to a process of instruction that encourages a close study of powerful writing and invites young writers to notice effective patterns they discover in the books they love while giving them a safe and supportive space to try those same patterns in their own writing.

But this wasn't the first time I'd encountered Jeff Anderson and his work.

I can still remember what I was wearing as I walked into the last classroom on the right on the first day of school. A sleeveless turquoise mock turtleneck. Floral printed culottes. Those are long shorts that look like a skirt if you're not familiar with early 90s fashion. I was also growing out a perm. Mr. Anderson might have been the tallest man I'd ever seen. He towered over all of us, but we could tell immediately. He was the fun fourth-grade teacher. Floppy hair, glasses, and occasionally, cowboy boots.

We spent that year together, learning about different cloud types, how to write in cursive, all the parts of the food chain, appositives, and compound sentences. He'd bound around the room, chalk in hand, notes scribbled on the board, talking loudly and gesturing wildly to hold our attention. I remember his excitement halfway through the year when he finally got a whiteboard. No more chalk dust.

And though it's been nearly three decades since we shared that classroom as teacher and student, we now share the pages of this very book. Mr. Anderson (who I guess I should start calling Jeff) continues to be my teacher as he is for many. He has given us an innovative approach to grammar instruction through invitations beginning with his book *Everyday Editing* and now in *Patterns of Power*.

A few years ago, as a fourth-grade teacher myself, I reconnected with Jeff at one of his trainings. I talked to him about how much I loved his book, *Everyday Editing,* which took students through an invitational process to deeply investigate certain conventions of language. I told him how I would do those lessons with my fourth graders in Spanish. We would use up nearly every sticky note I had as we looked for all the capital letters outside of the first word of the sentence we could find in my informational books. We would try to write the shortest sentences possible in Spanish as I adapted Jeff's lesson on simple sentences.

And when Jeff and Whitney published more than 70 lessons using the invitational process, elementary writing teachers everywhere felt like they had hit the jackpot. We now had *Patterns of Power* at our fingertips. We could take students through a series of invitations to help them discover conventions of language. It totally changed our grammar instruction.

We could ditch the copies of workbooks. The repetitive practice of writing sentences that use the same convention. The incorrect sentence we have to make correct.

Jeff and Whitney gave us the permission and resources to look at good sentences, excellent sentences, sentences with meaning and depth. They gave us the structure with which we could take a beautiful sentence and work with it over and over without losing interest. We could look at what authors actually do rather than what textbook makers think children can understand.

Now we're better prepared to listen to students and let them express what they know and what they notice about language. We value the knowledge our young writers bring into the classroom every day. They are no longer bound to a single right answer on a worksheet.

We put students into the role of the apprentice, learning from an author we know and trust. We examine craft in these lessons and give space for each child to play with language in their own writing. No red pens. No wrong answers. Only room to grow, to "try on" what a real-life author did.

And so we send them into the writer's workshop equipped with tools, valuing what they knew before the lesson and building their understanding even more.

Jeff's argument that we don't look at rules but rather at patterns is especially important for a classroom of students learning in two languages. We have found mentor sentences to lean on, and even fall back on if necessary. We value even the smallest attempts to replicate the use of the convention. We've lowered the risk of writing—possibly the hardest step in language acquisition. And all attempts are celebrated. What could be more important for language learning?

Patterns of Power changed the way I taught grammar in my classroom. As a bilingual educator working in a dual-language setting, English Language Arts was only half of my time. Spanish Language Arts was the other half. And there is no way I was going to do awesome lessons on conventions in English and then hand out a worksheet in Spanish.

This is nothing new for bilingual teachers in the United States. We frequently struggle to find equivalent lessons or activities in English and Spanish. We can find resources from Latin American countries. And at times we can find decent Spanish resources produced in the US. But we don't really find materials in both languages that are complementary, so we just piece it together ourselves.

In planning with my team we'd lay out our *Patterns of Power* books looking for the lessons that we knew our fourth graders needed. Simple sentences, compound sentences, commas in a series, adverbs, among other things. We'd flag the *Patterns of Power* lessons we wanted to teach in the following week. But we knew we'd have to write our own correlating lessons in Spanish.

Jeff states this in *Everyday Editing:*

> "I invite students to notice, to read like writers, to come into the world of editing—a friendly place rather than a punishing place, a creational facility rather than a correctional one. When we develop a place where concepts can be developed and patterns can be learned, kids feel safe, take risks, and feel welcome in every stage of the writing process." (Anderson 2007)

Jeff asks that we push kids to read like writers. But this requires something of us. We have to read like teachers of writing.

So that's what I started doing. Collecting. I looked for sentences in Spanish wherever I could find them. I had amassed a bilingual classroom library of over one thousand books in my thirteen years teaching fourth grade. I would take a few home every now and then. I'd keep a running list not only of sentences I found that I knew I could use to teach a particular concept but also just sentences I loved that I had no idea what I would teach with them. This must be how Jeff and Whitney started too—looking through the books they loved, the authors they loved, and thinking about the conventions they needed to teach.

Jeff and Whitney's lesson cycle works perfectly in Spanish. We go through the same steps no matter which language we are working in. We want students to notice and discover on their own. We can ask the same questions and follow their steps to do exactly the same thing *Patterns of Power* does in English—allow students to lead us through an examination of conventions and try out a convention in their own writing.

As I began developing lessons for my students based on *Patterns of Power*, I went through all the original lessons to identify which ones should have a Spanish equivalent. For example, capitalizing names of people needs a Spanish equivalent but capitalizing months and days doesn't. Then I started to look for what might be missing. What did I need to add or change to make sure I covered all my state standards regarding the conventions of writing in Spanish? I wrote those lessons for my students too.

We needed to work on how accents change meaning, how a sentence can be as small as one word, or how we punctuate dialogue in Spanish. We would talk about how magical Spanish is—that it has these special characteristics that are different from English. We would investigate the author's original use of conventions and then try it out in our own writing. Using Jeff and Whitney's lessons plus my own led to a classroom culture of reading as writers. The imbalance of resources was resolved. What I could teach in Spanish was just as interesting and enriching as what I could teach in English. And it was the first year that I felt I could forego the test prep and worksheets yet still have my classroom of kids prepared to take a state writing test in either language.

And it all began with an invitation to notice.

Prolific children's author Jane Yolen gives us this sentence in the historical fiction book *Encuentro* from the voice of a Taíno man reflecting on Columbus's arrival to his homeland.

Tomamos su idioma en nuestras bocas, olvidando el nuestro.
—Jane Yolen, *Encuentro*

What do you, the bilingual educator, notice?

¿Pronombres posesivos? ¿Sujetos tácitos? Maybe it's the content of the sentence that strikes you. Maybe you've heard kids say they have forgotten how to speak Spanish as they go through much of their day speaking English. Maybe you've sat with a parent or grandparent who complains that their child struggles to communicate in Spanish at home. Many students step into learning environments where English takes over and, unfortunately, occupies the space in the mind of a child where Spanish once resided.

That is precisely the outcome we, as bilingual teachers, hope to avoid. We teach in Spanish to make sure that the language of the home and family is not forgotten. We teach in Spanish so that children can develop fully their linguistic repertoires, communicate with the vast majority of people in the Western Hemisphere, and so they can find connections in their linguistically diverse communities.

By teaching in Spanish in your elementary classroom, you push back on a history where educational institutions once stripped students of home languages in favor of English. And here we are now, using both languages and valuing the language of the home as well as English. By doing this, we are indeed activating patterns of language that give each student the power to exercise their linguistic resources. Finding the patterns of language that writers employ grants students the power to use these same patterns to find their own voice and write their own stories.

You have picked up this book because you feel a commitment to value Spanish in your classroom. Simply by teaching in Spanish you are doing something liberating. You have decided that we have more power when we develop not just our English tongue but our Spanish language as well. You are allowing your students to discover that power as a community of bilingual writers.

The beautiful thing about Jeff and Whitney's lesson cycle is that the start of every lesson asks the children to speak first. Our job in this moment is to affirm and acknowledge that they are capable of noticing patterns in language. *En español.* We need to hear our students make sense of language. They need the time to do so. The power is theirs to discover.

1 Getting Started with the Patterns-of-Power Process

I can hear the murmurs in the classroom as we get started on a lesson on *sujetos tácitos*. As students whisper and point, I say, "Creo que ya conocen este libro . . ." and they erupt. They talk over one another to tell the story of what happens during the *tamalada*. María and her mother are making tamales for a Christmas gathering. She tries on her mother's wedding ring but loses the diamond ring in the *masa*. The family has to eat tons of tamales to find the ring. There is a happy ending for María and her mother. At this point, we arrive at what I was just about to teach: *sujetos tácitos*. And the subject, is precisely María and her mother.

What is it about the Gary Soto's *Too Many Tamales/¡Qué montón de tamales!* that pulls students in before we've even said a word, with just the title of a well-known book in our canon of Latino children's literature? It might be the parts of the story where the characters collaboratively prepare a traditional food that dates back to pre-Colombian México. It might be the eating of the tamales around Christmas time. Perhaps it is the feeling of family throughout the book. Or, it could just be the funny way that the problem of the missing ring is resolved. Whatever it is, children are already examining conventions of language and author's craft before we've even asked our first question.

In her essay "Windows and Mirrors and Sliding Doors," Rudine Sims Bishop (1990) talks about how our curriculum can offer windows in which we see characters and representations from cultures different from our own, and mirrors in which we see ourselves. Our students of color will likely have many "windows" throughout their educational journey. They will see many examples of how people unlike themselves live. They will hear language patterns and words that are unfamiliar to them. They will likely gain understanding and empathy toward others through these experiences.

But when do they get to see themselves? To know that their lived experiences are important and valued? To know that they are important enough to appear in books? To know that they are capable enough to write books? As bilingual educators, we have an obligation to provide many mirrors. Using literature that connects directly to students' lived experiences as we teach conventions is a great place to start.

Take for example, stories that feature different types of border crossing. When I started teaching, there were few books that mentioned border-crossing, and fewer still that alluded to undocumented border crossing. Yet in my classroom, this type of story was relevant to some students, many parents, and several extended family members of students in the class. The day we read Duncan Tonatiuh's *Pancho Rabbit and the Coyote* for the first time it took us over an hour. The students had so much to say, so many questions, but more than anything, so many connections. Perhaps they had never seen this story of undocumented crossing represented in their school experience up to that point. Perhaps there was safety and comfort in our class where almost every student could find a very personal connection to the book. From our discussions and the quick-writes they did after reading *Pancho Rabbit and the Coyote,* we pieced together a poem that included ideas from everyone. It was anonymous in that we named no one, yet very personal in that each student could find themselves in it. Students read this poem for Duncan Tonatiuh at our local book festival.

Our Journeys: A Multi-Voice Poem by Ms. Sweet's Class (2013)

I'm ten years old.

I'm in 4th Grade.

I live in the United States.

I always have.

I came here when I was a baby.

Yo vine hace dos años.

My parents grew up in the United States, but my family speaks Spanish.

My grandpa said they grew up very poor.

My dad said there was no work in Mexico

in Honduras

in Guatemala

My mom said we could go to school in the United States and have the education she didn't get to have.

My family decided that we would go.

My best friend told me how he swam across the river.

My mom told me how cold the water was and how she held me close because I was just a baby.

My dad said he crossed the desert. He said he had no food,

no water

no shoes

no money

That's how my tío died.

My mom tried to come three times before she got across. I waited for her for a year.

I came across at night.
We ran.
We were quiet.

We had nothing. Just the phone number of my cousin who would come pick us up.

Now we are here.

Some of us were born here.

Some of us were carried here as babies.

Some of us just came here. Apenas llegué.

But we all want the same thing.

To learn.

To grow.

To find our way.

I want to be a doctor.

I want to be a vet.

I want to be a teacher.

I want to be an artist.

I want to be an author.

Will you let me?

Since that moment, I decided to use every book I could find about undocumented crossing: *My Shoes and I* and *From North to South* by René Colato Laínez, *Two White Rabbits* by Jairo Buitrago, *Migrar* by José Manuel Mateo, *La Frontera* by Deborah Mills, *My Name is Jorge on Both Sides of the River* by Jane Medina, *Friends from the Other Side* by Gloria Anzaldúa. When I talk about this in professional development sessions, inevitably someone asks if it's too controversial for the classroom. I don't necessarily have the answer to that, but what I do know is that there is nothing controversial about getting to know your students very well and allowing them to find themselves and their families in literature. And though an outsider might find controversy in these literature choices, twenty-something 9- and 10-year-olds found a space to share their stories and their families' stories.

The number of books published each year about children of color by authors of color is far below where it should be. But bilingual teachers do what we have always done: search high and low for culturally-relevant texts and make them part of our teaching. That is why all the sentences throughout this book come from texts featuring children of color, reference an aspect of Latino culture, or are written by trusted authors. Our classroom libraries and our daily literary experiences then become a responsive, reflective way to teach the specific children in our classrooms.

In *Patterns of Power*, Jeff and Whitney give us a great bank of lessons from a wide variety of authors. Some of the books they use have Spanish translations. I've even translated Lola Shaefer's *An Island Grows* in my own handwriting, directly on the pages of the book, in order to teach Jeff's simple sentence lesson from *Everyday Editing*. Though it is possible to teach the conventions through translations, we know it's not enough. I could teach Lesson 5.2 from the original *Patterns of Power* (3.2 in this book), where we examine when to capitalize certain nouns and when not to, with a translation. I could probably find a translated copy of Kevin Henkes's *Chrysanthemum*, or *Crisantemo*, in my school's library. The lesson would probably be effective and quite engaging since students know Henkes's books well. But as a bilingual educator, I have another goal in my classroom beyond teaching the standards.

I want a classroom full of kids who see themselves as authors. I want to highlight authors who celebrate Latino culture and Spanish language. I want students to see that people with backgrounds similar to theirs grow up to become authors. In our classrooms, we can give these authors the rock-star status they deserve.

So instead of using *Crisantemo*, I choose a sentence from Jorge Argueta. He's an award-winning author. He writes poetry and stories for children that reflect his own immigrant experience as he left El Salvador to live in the United States and that celebrate his indigenous heritage and a reverence for nature.

In this way we accomplish a two part-goal: teach language conventions that are designated by our standards while showing children of color that people with similar backgrounds are authors to be celebrated. This is one of the primary ways we build our classroom community of bilingual writers. We place these bilingual authors and authors of color on a pedestal and aspire to be and write like them. They give kids permission to write about the day-to-day things that are most important to them.

It has been found that using culturally-relevant literature leads to better reading comprehension and development of a positive self-identity (Freeman and Freeman 2004). If we are working on *Patterns of Power* lessons for ten minutes each day, what better way to spend those ten minutes than with beautifully crafted sentences from authors of color with ideas that connect directly to students' lives?

Planning Lessons Using the Patterns-of-Power Process

In their book, Jeff and Whitney discuss in detail the Patterns-of-Power planning procedures and teaching conventions with an invitational process. This planning is essential: we think deeply about what students actually need to know and be able to do before designing our lessons. Aside from an enhanced obligation to carefully select literature that speaks to the lived experiences of our bilingual students, the process is the same in Spanish.

Figure 1.1
The *Patterns-of-Power* Planning Process

El proceso de planear las lecciones de Patterns of Power
I. Selecciona el estándar de aprendizaje.
II. Haz la conexión entre el propósito del autor y el uso del patrón gramatical.
III. Crea la frase de enfoque.
IV. Busca citas en la literatura que demuestran el propósito y el poder del patrón gramatical.

Selecting Your Standard

Selecting a convention or language standard is an obvious place to begin, but how do you decide which one to start with? You could review your students' writing and see what they need right now, or reflect on common struggles you have observed as a bilingual teacher over the years. You could also refer to local, state, or national standards. Though you'd think a standard would be fairly straightforward and classroom-ready, one standard may encompass multiple teaching goals. To illustrate, consider this first-grade standard from Texas.

> Edit drafts using standard Spanish conventions, including: singular, plural, common, and proper nouns, including gender-specific articles.

Even though you've selected a standard, you still have to decode what the standard actually asks elementary students to do. Since one standard can be stacked with multiple concepts, to teach particular patterns of language, we delve into each standard and sort out its smallest developmentally appropriate chunk. We ask ourselves the following questions, knowing that we'll build on a convention's concept over time:

- What's a digestible chunk for our grade level? Too many skills at once aren't manageable for elementary students. We start small and build on the concept in subsequent lessons. In the case of the standard that addresses the use of nouns above, we can start with the difference between common and proper nouns.
- *What do our writers need to know first?* For our focus on common and proper nouns with first graders, we decide on beginning with the feature that distinguishes common and proper nouns: the fact that we capitalize proper nouns. Beginning with capitalization of proper nouns helps readers see what function they serve as opposed to common nouns. It's a manageable instructional target.
- *What will our students need to know about the convention to gain meaning from it as both readers and writers?* We think how students will later apply the chosen standard in their own reading and writing. Kids don't need to deal with meaningless abstract terminology and definitions that hold no meaning or purpose for them. With this in mind, we'll make sure our instruction encourages writers to consider how they use common and proper nouns with an eye toward craft and meaning. In other words, we want our lesson to leave kids thinking less about what common and proper nouns are *called* and more about the job they actually *do*.
- *What connections do my students need to make between Spanish and English to build their bilingualism? How can I help them make those connections?* As we consider how best to help students develop as bilingual readers and writers, we anticipate in our planning the ways students can connect a concept across languages. There are a few concepts that are only found in one of the languages. But there are many that apply to both. In the case of common and proper nouns, capitalization is the distinguishing pattern that writers use in both English and Spanish. Since we are working with digestible chunks, we can build on certain differences between capitalization of nouns across English and Spanish in subsequent lessons (e.g., personal pronoun *I* vs. *yo*, months and days, languages and nationalities).

Linking the conventions of language to the art and craft of what authors do isn't always easy, but it is essential for real grammar instruction to occur over time. We continually connect the convention to the author's craft. In the next section, we'll explore moving conventions from correctness to a skill of communication, connecting these important patterns more deeply to author's craft and purpose—the *how* and the *why*.

Connect the Convention to Author's Purpose and Craft

Author's purpose *(el propósito del autor)* informs *why* writers do what they do, and writer's craft *(estilo del autor)* is *how* they do it. Writers craft their compositions in certain ways for clarity. They have a meaning-based reason for a convention's use. And writers need to know what effect conventions will have on a reader. For example, *signos de interrogación y ciertas palabras (quién, qué, cuándo, dónde, por qué y cómo)* affect how a reader reads their sentence. Their voice goes up at the end, ¿verdad?

Authors are powerful. They can make us do most anything they want. They can choose any pattern of power: *puntos finales, signos de interrogación, signos de admiración, conjunciones, comas, oraciones compuestas o complejas.* All of these moves affect how writing is read and how the reader makes and infers meaning.

In the end, the whole purpose of grammar and conventions instruction is to elevate writing. When determining what a standard is asking students to do, we think about how writers use it as a craft move. Aren't noun standards asking first-graders to know that the world is made up of people, places, things, and ideas that they already use in their writing? Try writing without nouns. It's impossible. Nouns are the stuff that writing is made of. And young writers come to understand this by writing and reading.

Writers show readers that a noun is proper by capitalizing it. For a first grader, proper nouns elevate writing with concrete detail and specificity. To speak about proper nouns at this level, we pivot from proper nouns to capitalization. We do this because capitalization is a digestible, concrete action that moves young writers to understand the difference between proper and common nouns on a basic level that's meaningful to them.

Pondering a convention's intended effect on a reader can unlock the *why*. And when students know *why* a convention is used—*su propósito*—they will be able to comprehend its meaning while reading and create meaningful effects while writing—that is, they'll be able to practice the craft or *desarrollar su estilo del autor*. They'll also gain the knowledge needed to edit for the convention's correct usage when they make a mistake in their own compositions, which invariably happens. In short, once writers understand a convention's purpose and craft, they know how to use it. It's not just some rule to prattle off with no understanding. It's part of what they do to write.

Create a Focus Phrase

Once young writers have uncovered the convention and they begin to understand why and how authors use it, we create a focus phrase. The term *focus phrase* comes from Terry Thompson's book *The Construction Zone* (2015). A focus phrase helps teachers and students commit to a concise and manageable learning target, such as, *Uso la letra mayúscula al inicio de los nombres y apellidos de personas.* The focus phrase needs to be brief, so students will be able to say it and internalize it. Additional benefits of the focus phrase become evident throughout the writing and teaching process because the statement

- keeps the teacher focused on the instructional goal during planning and delivery,
- maintains student focus on the goal throughout the instruction, and
- becomes a source for students' self-talk when they are working independently and eventually becomes their independent thought.

But focus phrases will mean nothing to students unless they see the convention used in the context of authentic writing. So, we suggest you share the focus phrase only after a mentor or model text has been displayed and students in some way notice the focus convention within the sentence. Since we teach by responding to students' noticings, finding a model sentence that demonstrates the focus convention is essential.

Curate a Small Bit of Writing That Demonstrates the Conventions Power and Purpose

After we've defined our focus phrase, the next planning component is to find a model text that showcases the convention in action. Remember, making the lesson narrow directs students' attention to a particular convention. Often one sentence is adequate to demonstrate a skill or standard in context, but from time to time, more than one sentence may be needed to model a particular skill or give sufficient context. For example, teaching conventions of dialogue may require three or four paragraphs to show multiple conventions in action.

Whenever possible, the writing should come from a piece of literature that uses Spanish in an authentic way. We look for books originally written in Spanish or by bilingual authors. We look for books with characters that look like the children in our classrooms. And we look for beautiful sentences that draw us into a lesson. Be cautious here and be selective. It's not uncommon to find excerpts in our bilingual books that either don't adhere to the Spanish pattern for that particular convention or try to apply English grammar structures to the Spanish text. These texts can certainly come up in other parts of instruction. But because our focus is so narrow, we want to use excerpts that are written correctly and follow the expected grammatical patterns.

Juan Felipe Herrera's books can be found in many bilingual classrooms. He served as the US Poet Laureate from 2015 to 2017. *The Upside-Down Boy* is a well-known book in Latino children's literature and beyond. The story tells about Herrera's experience as he starts school not speaking English but finds he enjoys writing poetry with the help of a kind teacher. Choosing a sentence from this book is perfect for first-graders.

> *Ella le enseña mi pintura a doña Andasola quien* se
> *la muestra* a *Gabino, su canario.*

I chose this sentence because of the multiple uses of proper nouns, including first and last names. When we use authentic writing, young readers and writers will likely notice more than the focus skill. And that's okay. The additional conventions may not be the focus of the lesson, but teaching in context is about showing how language works together to create meaning. At a minimum, seeds are planted or awareness is activated about a future focus or we can spiral back to previous learnings.

Even though each lesson in this book includes possible sentences, craft connections, and focus phrases, I still strongly recommend talking through author's purpose and craft links with colleagues before jumping into instruction. You'll find your lessons are more flexible and effective when you take the time for this important step of planning and clarifying the learning target, focus phrase, and model text.

The Invitational Process: Activating the Power of Your Plan

Once the plan is in place, we teach and interact with students through a set of invitations. Now that we've deepened our awareness of what we're teaching, we've also bolstered our trust in ourselves, students, and the process. The process will unfold easily as we invite students to interact with a mentor text in various ways.

We launch the model sentence and stand back and wait for our students' reactions, and then we build upon their noticings. They will guide us to the next place instructionally. We'll never be prepared for all their noticings, but as long as we honor their attempts at making meaning, together we can learn how the complexities of language unfold in both predictable and unpredictable patterns. Here, we take a look at a Spanish lesson on capitalizing names in action, which highlights the steps of the invitational process that specifically invite writers to *notice*, *compare*, *imitate*, *celebrate*, *apply* and *edit* (see Figure 1.2).

Figure 1.2
The Patterns-of-Power Invitational Process

- La invitación a NOTAR
  Usamos una oración de la literatura para enseñar un concepto de la gramática en español. La lección siempre empieza con la pregunta: "¿Que notan en esta oración?"
- La invitación a COMPARAR
  Estudiamos una imitación justamente debajo de la oración original. La conversación empieza con las preguntas: "¿En que se parecen? ¿En que son diferentes?"
- La invitación a IMITAR
  Usando las oraciones que hemos estudiado en clase como guía, los escritores intentan emplear el patrón de poder en la escritura con el apoyo del maestro o los compañeros de clase. Cuando están listos, los estudiantes pueden intentar usar el patrón independientemente.
- La invitación a CELEBRAR
  Los estudiantes comparten su escritura con los compañeros de clase para celebrar su intento.
- La invitación a APLICAR
  El patrón es usado para responder a la literatura, revisar su propio trabajo escrito o de otra manera significativa para el estudiante.
- La invitación a CORREGIR
  Los estudiantes estudian cuatro versiones

¿Qué notas?: An Invitation to Notice in Action

When we display a sentence from one of our favorite bilingual books that shows how we capitalize names, we assure students that the sentence is correct so they don't immediately try to fix it. "Este año vamos a ver las oraciones más bonitas que encontramos en los libros. Queremos saber qué hacen los autores con las palabras y la puntuación para expresar sus ideas. Vamos a aprender cómo nosotros lo podemos hacer." Then we ask them the essential question that starts every lesson, "¿Qué notas?"

In a classroom of bilingual first graders with varying levels of English and Spanish, I display Juan Felipe Herrera's sentence. I've chosen this sentence to emphasize the difference between common nouns and proper nouns—that we use a capital letter to distinguish between the two.

Figure 1.3

Ella le enseña mi pintura a doña Andasola quien se la muestra a Gabino, su canario.

–Juan Felipe Herrera, *El niño de cabeza*

I read the sentence aloud twice, asking students to join on the second reading. After reading the sentence from the two-time poet laureate, I ask, "¿Qué notan?" And I wait.

I have students gathered together on the carpet and lean in to listen to what they say to their partners. I let students take their time, pausing, not talking, as students take the lead. But sometimes there is silence. Let it happen as readers' eyes scan the sentence.

"Hay un punto." A favorite response. Though it comes up in almost every lesson, I validate it each time.

"¿Qué hace este punto? ¿Qué nos dice el punto al final de la oración?" I ask, though I've asked it before. I'll probably ask it again to this same group of first graders the next day and perhaps the next. Although end punctuation isn't the focus of this particular lesson, we want to validate students' observations about the sentence. And we know very well that most elementary students need frequent review of the function of the period.

"El punto nos dice que paramos."

I put my hand out indicating a stop. "¡Alto!"

I invite students to hold out their arms with me. "¿Qué nos dice el punto?"

"¡Alto!" We shout with our hands out.

"Ahora sabemos que ya se terminó la oración y podemos empezar otra oración."

¿Qué más?

Wait time is essential after posing the question, "¿Qué notas?" But as students start to offer ideas, the next equally important question is, "¿Qué más?" With this follow-up, wait time continues to be imperative. If I begin to speak, I end up driving the lesson. After waiting at least fifteen seconds, we can follow up with other questions:

- ¿Alguien sabe qué hace este signo de puntuación?
- ¿De qué otra manera podemos explicar lo que dijo Raúl?
- ¿Hay algo que vean en lo que tengan dudas?

A first grader notes that there is more than one capital letter in this sentence from *El niño de cabeza.* So, I ask, "¿Qué letras son las letras mayúsculas?"

Several students point out the three capital letters.

"¿Cómo sabemos que estas son las letras mayúsculas?"

"Porque son más grandes."

I touch the letters on the chart gauging their size. "Sí, son más grandes."

At this point, we use two questions to push students to think about a certain convention.

Figure 1.4

By using these two questions, students build a theory about the function of the convention. We listen to their thoughts. We highlight, extend, and connect to them, adding explicit information when needed, and in doing so, enrich their understanding of the convention's function.

"¿Qué hacen las letras mayúsculas al leer la oración en voz alta?" I prompt. After about fifteen seconds, I reread the sentence from *El niño de cabeza* aloud and say. "Parece que las letras mayúsculas no hacen mucho al leerlas en voz alta. Cuando leo las palabras con letras mayúsculas, no tengo que hacer una pausa, respirar, o cambiar mi voz."

The kids continue examining the sentence.

"¿Qué hacen las letras mayúsculas al leer la oración con solamente los ojos?" I make a production of reading the sentence silently. My first graders scan the sentence, too.

"Es que las letras mayúsculas están paradas y las letras minúsculas están sentadas," a student explains.

"Entonces podemos decir que las letras mayúsculas resaltan más que las otras letras." The students agree. I continue, "Los autores usan las letras mayúsculas solamente cuando hay una razón. Vamos a ver las letras mayúsculas en esta oración."

I point to the first word in the sentence. "¿Por qué esta palabra empieza con una letra mayúscula?"

"Es la primera letra de la oración."

"Así que una de las razones de por qué un autor usa las letras mayúsculas es para empezar una oración." Students agree with the assertion.

"Pero parece que Juan Felipe Herrera usó letras mayúsculas por otra razón aquí." I point to the capital letters in the middle of the sentence.

"Son nombres," Gabriela says.

"Así es. Los escritores siempre usan letras mayúsculas en nombres y apellidos." I write the focus phrase on chart paper. "Uso letras mayúsculas al inicio de los nombres y apellidos de personas."

Here, I read the focus phrase and the class repeats it. I've saved the focus phrase for this moment when students begin to see it on their own. After the focus convention is discovered, we work in the phrase as much as possible throughout the lesson, the day, and the week.

"*Andasola* lleva una letra mayúscula porque es su apellido." Ana says.

"*Gabino* es el nombre de su pajarito."

"Entonces los escritores usan letras mayúsculas en los nombres de las personas y las mascotas," I affirm.

"¿Pero por qué *doña* no tiene una letra mayúscula?" Alex asks.

¿En qué se parecen? ¿En qué se diferencian?: An Invitation to Compare and Contrast in Action

I've anticipated that this might come up and have to decide if I want to address this now or save it for tomorrow? This is the risk we take when we ask the kids to guide us through the lesson. "Ojos de águila. Es interesante que *doña* no lleva letra mayúscula."

I've made sure that the *invitación a comparar* has a different title we use for showing respect for a person. This sentence closely follows the structure of Juan Felipe Herrera's original sentence. I write both sentences on the chart.

Ella le enseña mi pintura a doña Andasola quien se la muestra a Gabino, su canario.

Él le enseñó mi tarea a la Sra. Gómez quien se la mostró al Sr. Rodríguez, el director.

"¿En qué se parecen? ¿En qué se diferencian?" I ask.

In pairs, students analyze the mentor text and its imitation—orally, in writing, or both. This collaborative conversation deepens students' consciousness of the standard and its effect, laying the groundwork for later application. As they do this, we repeat our focus phrase, *Uso letras mayúsculas al inicio de los nombres y apellidos de personas*.

I ask Alex and his partner to remember the question Alex asked yesterday about the word *doña*. They are ready to discuss as the class returns to the carpet and chart paper to do some heavy analysis.

"*Señor* y *señora* tienen letras mayúsculas." Alex shares.

The class nods that he is indeed correct.

"Es como *Ms.* in English," Daniel says.

I have to decide how much I want to discuss with first graders the varied titles that we can give people to show respect. The lesson is on capitalizing names, but since students are already jumping in, I decide to follow their lead.

Figure 1.5

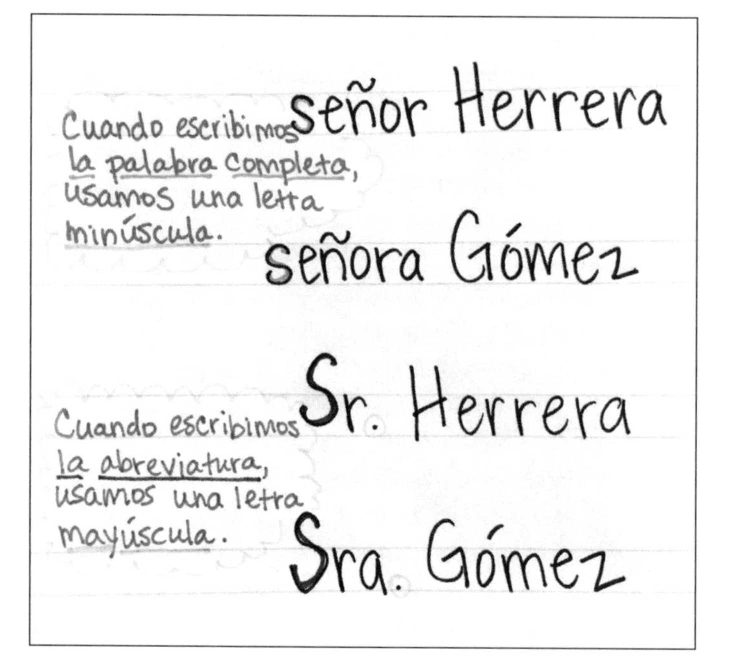

I write *señor* and its abbreviation on a piece of chart paper. "¿Cómo se dice esta palabra? ¿Y esta?" Students say *señor* for both. "Se pronuncian iguales. ¿En qué otra manera se parecen?" Students say that they begin and end with the same letters.

"¿En qué se diferencian?" I prod.

"Uno es cortito," Alondra notices.

"Uno tiene un punto," Jaime says.

"Usamos un punto cuando escribimos ciertas palabras con su forma corta."

I point to *Sr. Rodríguez*. "Necesitamos el punto para indicar que estamos usando su forma corta. Se llama una abreviatura.Y cuando usamos su forma corta, necesitamos . . ."

"¡Un punto!" the class responds.

Don't be afraid of what kids may notice or wonder. Eventually you'll learn to use whatever they say with ease to drive forward their curiosity and engagement. You manage how much time is spent on what. You decide the focus phrase and pick the sentence. In planning, you've set everything up for these young bilingual writers to discover and learn about the Spanish language. Let them share what they notice or wonder about the sentence or sentences displayed—questions, punctuation identification, or whatever they observe. They'll surprise you.

Even though capitalizing titles used with last names to show respect isn't the target standard, we allow for the organic process to unfold. When kids are curious about meaning, we follow that interest, engaging them deeply, our explanations springing forth from their wonderings.

Inténtalo: An Invitation to Imitate in Action

To this point, writers have explored a model sentence, discovered its pattern of power, connected it to a focus phrase, and compared and contrasted it with an imitation. It's time for them to apply the convention by composing a similar sentence. This is the practical application that grammar research supports (Graham and Perrin 2007). Imitation provides a natural way to bring best-practice and research-based methods to convention and grammar instruction. This part of the lesson is especially impactful for our bilingual students for whom taking risks in language often leads to significant learning. Through imitation, we create a low-risk, highly-scaffolded opportunity to experiment with language conventions, whether students are working in their first or second language.

You have several options for imitating the model sentence:

- Shared writing
- Interactive writing
- Paired writing
- Independent writing

This menu of imitation choices ranges from most-teacher-supported (shared writing) to least-teacher-supported (independent writing). You may choose to do all of these variations in order over a few days or choose just the ones appropriate for your students' needs. Imitation can take more than one ten-minute block over more than one day if you choose. Let the complexity or the skill and the student needs dictate that decision.

In general, when imitating a pattern, we follow the steps show in Figure 1.6.

As writers, it's crucial that we build a habit of rereading our writing. Quite often we need to make adjustments. That's revision. That's editing. That's writing. Writers read and reread their own writing with their reader's eyes and their writer's eyes, even when it's just a sentence, and most of the time they tinker with it (See Figure 1.7].

Figure 1.6
The Steps to Imitating a Pattern

En la invitación a imitar...
- Repasa las oraciones en la invitación a notar y la inivitación a comparar.
- Usa los ojos de lector para observar los patrones del autor.
- Observa el mundo con los ojos del escritor—piensa en personas, lugares y tus experiencias.
- Intenta usar el patrón del autor para expresar tus propias ideas.
- Relee tu oración (u oraciones) en voz alta para asegurarte de que tenga sentido.

Figure 1.7

At this point we're in the middle of the year with first graders. They are used to shared writing in this part of the lesson cycle. In shared writing the teacher models, holding the pen. But I've decided this group is ready for a semi-supported imitation choice to begin: interactive writing. Interactive writing is like shared writing in that we compose a sentence together as a class combining ideas to try out the author's pattern. In interactive writing, the students take turns holding the pen (marker in this case). Young writers share ideas, and the teacher orally helps students combine their ideas to make a cohesive sentence. Students guide each other in this collaborative method of composing a sentence. This way, students find the support of their peers as they try out the pattern of the author.

"Usen los ojos de lectores para ver la oración de Juan Felipe Herrera. ¿Qué hizo?"

"Usó letras mayúsculas," Andrés says.

"¿Por qué usó las letras mayúsculas?" I wait.

"Porque son nombres de personas," several students respond.

"Repitan conmigo, 'Uso letras mayúsculas al inicio de los nombres y apellidos de personas.'"

I walk over to the chart with the original sentence. "Juan Felipe Herrera escribió de una pintura que hizo. ¿Qué es algo que les gustaría enseñar a alguien más?" Students discuss toys, drawings, homework, new shoes, and books. Then they discuss the people around them that they could show those things to.

I listen to their ideas and remind students that it's okay if their idea isn't used, as they will soon get to craft their own sentence.

After the children come to some agreements on the content of the sentence, I ask them to come to the chart paper individually to add in parts of the sentence. The result is a collaboratively crafted sentence, edited with peer-support in the moment. Students teach each other on where capital letters should go.

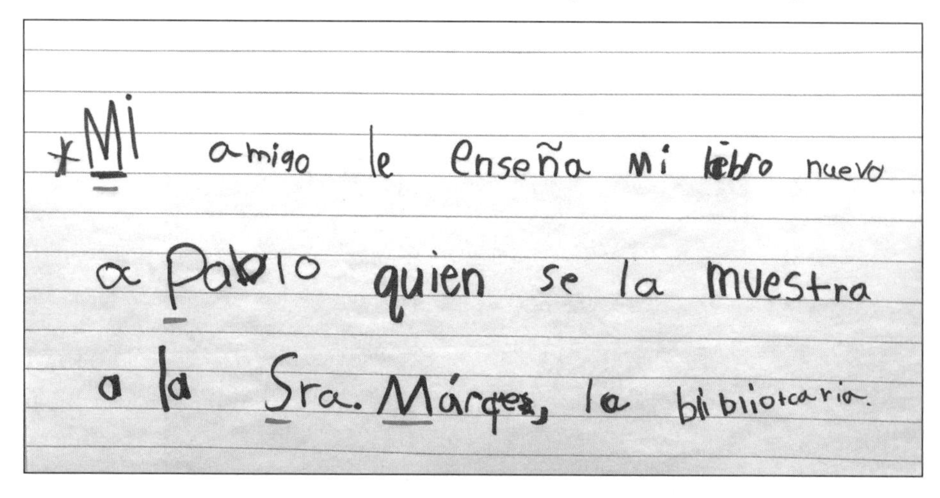

Remind students of the focus phrase as you review the sentence with them. After you have worked through a shared or interactive writing imitation, you may choose to use paired or independent writing the next day. Decide based on the complexity of the task, student engagement, and need.

In some cases, you may choose to move right to paired or independent writing which gives the students the most responsibility. If you do this and find that it is not working, you can always go back a step. But I often find that students are ready to write their own sentences, some doing it before they are even asked. The important thing is for students to try the convention, reaching into possibility.

Once paired or independent writing is completed, it begs to be shared. This is one of the most important components of the process: celebration. It can happen the same day the imitation sentences are written or the next day, depending on the timing in your classroom.

¡Celebramos!: An Invitation to Celebrate in Action

After students have had a chance to imitate the original model sentence in pairs or independently, it's time for some celebration! Debbie Miller says, "What is celebrated gets repeated." But how often do we celebrate grammar in Spanish? Bilingual writers are often more likely to hear corrections than clapping, and if that's what we model, that's what students will do as well.

Instead, we want to imbue positive feelings and associations in our writers' experience with conventions and language learning. We focus on the illumination of the pattern rather than the eradication of error. This anchors student experiences in what writers do rather than mistakes they could make. To move in this direction, we make time to share students' imitations with an audience and celebrate their efforts. As writing process teachers, we know the importance of sharing and audience, so we allow as many kids to share as we reasonably can.

During our sharing discussions and celebrations, we deepen our understanding of the convention's use and see how the pattern connects across topics. As we hear other's sentences, we hear possibility. We hear the choices writers make. When the celebration is skipped because of time, or we've forgotten the power behind sharing in various ways, we miss a perfect opportunity for bilingual writers to honor risks and inspire each other.

Though all this best practice is also the best test practice you can get, the next invitation builds a bridge between good teaching and how the pattern may look on the test in an intentional way.

Corregimos: An Invitation to Edit in Action

Editing their own writing is the main skill we want young writers to master, but like it or not, they will also face standardized tests, benchmarks, and other situations with multiple-choice editing and grammar questions. Practice comes only after instruction—we believe we should err on the side of building concepts and deep understanding of the patterns of power in authentic literacy instruction.

Thus far in the invitation process, we have emphasized investigating effective and correct sentences. In fact, we go to great lengths to avoid the study of incorrect writing. We still don't overwhelm students with errors at this point. For the bulk of this process, students have been soaked in correctness and effectiveness and beauty. They know and understand the concepts behind the conventions' moves and have applied them to their own compositions. In addition to the best practice, we can, at certain marker points such as nearing the end of our formal study of a convention, give young writes multiple versions of the same section of text, some of which will have one error. This type of practice should in no way replace or crowd out the actual teaching of conventions. For far too long, practice has passed for instruction. And they're not the same. Here's our suggestion for a way to link to tests.

Although the invitation process has been preparing writers for this hurdle of test questions through sound instruction, we can explicitly reinforce students' ability to transfer what they know to testing. How do we sharpen students' editing eyes, helping them spot how little changes affect meaning?

On tests, students have to spot minuscule errors sometimes as small as a comma or an accent mark, and to help them do that, we first build our knowledge of what the powerful patterns look like and mean. Then we can, from time to time, practice in a format aligned to how they'll be questioned on standardized tests.

On most standardized tests, a highlighted sentence or section of text is presented in four ways as a multiple-choice question. Each answer option includes subtle shifts in grammar decisions a writer might make that affect the meaning of the sentence, with only one option being correct. For this reason, we structure the invitation to edit *(Invitación a corregir)* in a way that presents three sentences with slight changes that affect meaning.

In the *Invitación-a-corregir* part of the process, we start by reviewing the correct, effective version of the sentence we studied and asking, "What did we learn about writing from the author?" We know the correct sentence won't always be the first on the test. But we're teaching, not testing.

Then, we investigate the three sentences with errors one at a time. In a first grade classroom, I uncover the correct version of the sentence from *El niño de cabeza.*

Ella le enseña mi pintura a doña Andasola quien se la muestra a Gabino, su canario.

"¿Qué aprendimos de Juan Felipe Herrera acerca de la escritura?" I ask. The correct sentence is presented first to give us an opportunity to review and restate what we have learned from the particular pattern of power or mentor sentence. Students generate recollections of what they specifically learned about writing from the author, telling what they know about the conventions of Spanish they've been studying. As this occurs, I emphasize the focus phrase.

"Aprendimos que usamos letras mayúsculas en los nombres."

"¿Todas las letras deben ser mayúsculas?" I ask.

"¡No!" several students chime in.

"Solo la primera."

And we repeat the focus phrase, "Uso letras mayúsculas al inicio de los nombres y apellidos de personas."

Next, we look at the incorrect sentences one at a time, much as one would on a standardized test, and at each sentence, we ask, "¿Qué ha cambiado? ¿Cuál es el efecto del cambio?" This takes careful, close reading. To begin, I cover the correct sentence and uncover the second sentence, which has one change:

Ella le enseña mi pintura a doña andasola quien se la muestra a Gabino, su canario.

After revealing the second version, I ask, "¿Qué cambió?"

We don't ask kids to focus on the mistake or error. We ask them to find what changed and how that change affects meaning.

A student notices that *Andasola* isn't capitalized.

"¿Y eso sí es importante?" I ask the class. The editing eyes first notice differences, and then they consider how the meaning is affected by the change. Writing isn't about right and wrong: it's about communicating meaning and effect in any language. If appropriate, after the change is identified, ask something along the lines of "¿Cuál es el efecto del cambio?"

The hope is that young writers will return to the focus phrase, but if they don't, I keep nudging it in. "Digan la frase conmigo: Uso letras mayúsculas al inicio de los nombres y apellidos de personas."

I may even go through every word in the sentence, asking if it should or shouldn't be capitalized. Each time I ask, "¿Cómo saben?" I do this until I feel the momentum dropping, and then we're off to the next version of the sentence. This one is covered and the next version is revealed.

Ella le enseña mi pintura a Doña Andasola quien se la muestra a Gabino, su canario.

"¿Qué cambió?" I ask.

"Doña tiene letra mayúscula," Kevin points out.

"No me importa. Así lo voy a escribir," I shrug.

"Así no es el patrón." Kevin points to the note with *señor* and *Sr.*

"Escribes letra mayúscula cuando es cortito y tiene un punto." Henry adds.

"Una abreviatura . . . Entonces no es necesario escribir *doña* con una letra mayúscula y no hay una abreviatura para *doña,* ya que es una palabra corta."

I uncover the last sentence, covering the one we've been working on.

Ella le enseña mi pintura a doña Andasola quien se la muestra a gabino, su canario.

The students study the sentence.

"Gabino no tiene mayúscula." Alejandra notes.

I repeat the focus phrase. "Gabino no es una persona."

"Pero es el nombre de su pajarito y usamos letras mayúsculas en los nombres," Alejandra counters.

"¿Hasta en los nombres de los pajaritos?" I ask.

The students agree. We must capitalize even the names of our pets.

As I close the discussion to begin writing workshop, I encourage the students to keep noting the capitalization of names the rest of the day and week. As we've discussed earlier, we invite students to reread their writer's notebook or journal entries, scrounging for words that need to be capitalized or should be capitalized. We only use capital letters for a reason.

Remember, there's a place for test practice, but it's a very thin slice of the instructional pie. In fact, overreliance on test preparation actually weakens performance. It's easy to grow weary of *test* practice replacing the best-practice instruction that makes students successful. If students know a convention well, they will be able to spot meaning problems in sentences and choose the best answer on a test. But to really own the convention, they need opportunities to take responsibility for using it in real drafts, and when they don't, for making adjustments. In small doses of conversations around authentic writing and lots of room for practice, the invitational process will move writers in that direction.

How Do You Make an Invitation to Edit?

Though this resource includes invitations to edit for each lesson, they're easy to make if you want to highlight new sentences your class is reading, writing, or studying.

- Type the sentence or sentences studied throughout the invitational process.
- Copy the sentence.
- Paste the copy of the sentence three times beneath the correct one for four versions of the sentences, total.
- Leave the first sentence as it is—correct.
- Change one convention in each of the three sentences beneath the correct one. What kinds of conventions do you change? Of course, you can change the convention you're showcasing. For instance, if you're working on capitalizing proper nouns, you could change a capital letter to lower case, or change a lower case letter to a capital. You can also use our students' common errors to drive the editing items. You could also change conventions outside your focus area if it would help writers deepen their awareness about this type of error.

Young writers develop an editing eye, deepening an awareness of how minor changes affect meaning. This is what they need to be prepared for as test takers, and it just so happens it helps us clean up our own writing as well.

Planning Possibilities for Your Classroom

As you move beyond planning one lesson to planning how to sequence a series of *Patterns of Power* lessons in a bilingual classroom, I suggest you lay out both books. If you are a bilingual or dual language teacher who teaches language arts in both languages, you couldn't possibly get through all of Jeff and Whitney's lessons and all the Spanish lessons in the year. But you wouldn't need to either. There are many skills that overlap and depending on the needs of your students, understanding of the convention and its power might come after a single lesson or two. In both languages, we start sentences with a capital letter and end with a period, our parts of speech have the same functions, and our verbs have to agree with our nouns, for example.

Based on your program model and the needs of the kids in your classroom, you will have to decide how to find a balance of English *Patterns of Power* lessons and Spanish ones. Our ultimate goal is that young writers can fully develop each of their linguistic repertoires and fluidly express themselves in either language. We hope that they will be able to make decisions regarding which language they use in writing based on the intended audience. We want to provide them with the tools to clearly and effectively communicate ideas in both languages.

As bilingual teachers, we know there will never be enough resources. We will always be asking for more. While our colleagues that teach in English easily find resources stacked in closets or on the Internet, those of us who teach in Spanish will always long for more, because our students deserve more. So we will do what bilingual teachers have always done. Be resourceful, and make our own. This book gives you a solid start. In time, you'll be ready to make your own Spanish lessons, that build on mine, and take your kids where they need to be.

When you're ready to start planning your own lessons, simply revisit the Patterns-of-Power Planning Process and the Invitational Process with your text and focus conventions in mind. Use the Spanish adaptation of the blank planning template found in Appendix A or the chart in Figure 1.9 to guide you as you explore the standard, consider *how* and *why* writers might use it, and connect all this thinking across both languages. Once you have your goal, model sentence, and focus phrase in mind, take a few moments to plan out how you'll lead your young writers through the steps of invitational process and go for it. You'll find yourself confident and up to speed in not time at all.

Planning Patterns-of-Power Lessons in Spanish	
Standard/Skill	Review your students' writing samples, reflect on common struggles you see each year, or refer to standards or skills. Choose a standard or skill and break it down by uncovering what it asks the writer to do.
Building Bilingualism	Consider how the same concept is similar or different to English. Keeping in mind students' proficiency in either language, create questions that draw students' attention to the similarities and differences of the languages.
Author's Purpose/ Craft	Connect the convention to the author's purpose (*why* writers do what they do) and craft (*how* they do it).
Focus Phrase	Create a focus phrase: kid-friendly language that states a clearly defined learning goal. Ex: *Uso una letra mayúscula al principio de una oración.*
Mentor Sentence/ Invitation to Notice	Curate a small bit of writing that demonstrates the convention's power and purpose by searching through literature that reflects your students' lived experiences.
Invitation to Compare and Contrast	Create an imitation of the mentor so that students can compare and contrast the two.
Invitation to Imitate Together	Decide if this imitation will be experienced through shared writing, interactive writing, or paired writing.
Invitation to Imitate Independently	Decide how the students will imitate independently (e.g., notebook, sentence strips, note cards, class book, etc.).
Invitation to Celebrate	Decide how the imitations will be celebrated while bringing back the focus phrase (e.g., class book, hang on wall, document camera, graffiti wall, etc.).
Invitation to Apply	Decide how you will extend the work throughout the day in other areas. What opportunities will the writer have to apply the skill?
Invitation to Edit	Copy and paste the sentence three times beneath the original sentence. Change one thing in each of the pasted sentences to lead a discussion about how the author's message is changed or affected by the change.

Pacing Possibilities for Your Classroom

Jeff and Whitney suggest that you could do a lesson spaced out over several days in ten-minute increments (See Figure 1.10). But sometimes we're having so much fun we end up spending more than ten minutes on our *Patterns of Power* lessons. How long you spend each day will depend on the age of your students and the schedule restraints that may exist in your school. Fourth and fifth graders might get through an entire lesson in two ten-minute chunks. Whereas our youngest writers might take two weeks. Remember that we need to hear students and adjust our pacing to allow for them to fully participate and engage.

Possible Schedule for Daily 10-Minute Invitations	
DAY	**Invitation to . . .**
1	Notice
2	Compare and Contrast
3	Imitate with Interactive or Shared Writing
4	Imitate as a Pair
5	Celebrate (Celebrating can be as simple as students reading their sentences aloud or displaying them on a document camera.)
6	Imitate Independently
7	Celebrate (Sharing on wall charts or class books could go on for more than a day.)
8	Edit

Let's look at an example of how this book can be used along with Jeff and Whitney's resources to create a series of lessons where we build understanding of a certain convention across English and Spanish. In this case, we look at teaching commas in a series.

Lesson 1	Lesson 2	Lesson 3	Lesson 4	Lesson 5
Introduce the concept in Spanish *Coma para separar elementos en una serie* Use lesson 14.1 in *PoP en español*	**Build on the concept in Spanish** *Coma para separar elementos en una serie* Use lesson 14.2 in *PoP en español*	**Build on the concept in Spanish** *Coma para separar elementos en una serie* Use lesson 14.3 in *PoP en español*	**Assess the concept in Spanish:** This can come from the lesson. The students' imitation might be the way you assess understanding. You might also use the *Invitación a corregir* or the *Invitación a aplicar.*	**Connect to English** Look at the original lessons for using commas in a series in Chapter 19 in Jeff and Whitney's lesson sets. Choose the lesson that is at the most appropriate level for your students. Remember your goal is to draw attention to the difference between English and Spanish patterns of punctuating items in a series or list.

When we are discussing items in a list in both English and Spanish we employ commas and a conjunction just before the last item. The only difference is that in Spanish we do not use the comma before the conjunction between the penultimate and last item (in English, you might compare this to the use of the Oxford comma). That's it. The skills we teach in one language can and do transfer to the other language. We don't have to teach Lesson 4.1 on capitalizing names twice. The rules are the same in both languages. We make a choice regarding the language of instruction for these foundational concepts according to our students or our bilingual program model. But we also make deliberate choices to show students how what they have learned in one language transfers to the other. There are, however, certain skills that just don't transfer as they are specific to one language or the other. Writing accents that affect pronunciation will only come up in Spanish, for example. These lessons will have to be taught on their own.

You'll find several supports to help you connect the Spanish lessons from this resource to their English counterparts in *Patterns of Power*. Chapter correlation notes are included in each chapter opener of this book and for an overview of all these lessons and how they connect to the English lessons in *Patterns of Power*, see the chart included in Appendix B.

Let's look at a skill that is important in English but is less important in Spanish: contractions. Contractions exist in Spanish, but there are only two. In English, we have many and it's a standard that appears across grade levels. This might be a concept you choose to introduce in English over the course of several lessons, as the concept is quite complex in English. Once bilingual students have shown that they understand the concept in English, you can use Lesson 11.3 from this book to help them notice the differences between contractions in English and contractions in Spanish.

Lesson 1	Lesson 2	Lesson 3	Lesson 4
Introduce the concept in English *Contractions* Use lesson 9.3 from the original *Patterns of Power* over two days.	**Build on the concept in English** *Apostrophes for contractions and ownership* Use lesson 9.1 in the original *Patterns of Power*.	**Assess the concept in English** This can come from the lesson. The students' imitation might be the way you assess understanding. You might also use the Invitation to Edit or the Invitation to Apply.	**Connect to Spanish** *Contractions in Spanish.* Use Lesson 11.3 in this book to look at the two contractions that exist in Spanish. Compare and contrast English conventions to Spanish conventions.

A note about the assessment that comes up before a concept is taught in the other language: This does not have to be a traditional assessment. It could easily occur during the lesson as you gauge students' understanding of the concept. If the imitation or application part of the lesson is still difficult for students, take the time to build their understanding in one language before linking to the other language.

Your planning should as often as possible arise from your students' needs. Once you've become used to the *Patterns of Power* process, you'll regularly look at our students' writing and immediately start thinking about invitations that could push them to grow as writers. And even though you are bound to your state standards, give yourself permission to be flexible, moving back and forth between this book and the original *Patterns of Power* in English. Lay out both books as you plan. Find lessons that build on one another and look for the opportunities to connect to the other language. But know that you don't always have to teach an English lesson for every Spanish lesson. Your students will let you know through their speaking, reading, and writing what they need in each language. Take their cues and take your time through lessons. You might complete one in a day. You might complete one lesson over the course of a week (or more). With every lesson let your students to guide you through, staying ready to listen and follow their lead.

Y tú y yo aprendimos a leer, a hablar, a escribir, y a hacer oír nuestras voces.

Somos historias.
Somos dos lenguas . . .

Yuvi Morales, *Soñadores*

Yuyi Morales reminds us that we must read, talk, and write to make our voices heard. It is through a deep understanding of language and how writers leverage their knowledge of language patterns that we put students into an apprenticeship with authors we know, love, and trust. We trust even our youngest writers to take on these patterns of power and use them to say the things they want to say, to make their voices, however small, heard.

We give them the tools we call conventions, not to trap them into an inescapable pattern that must be followed every time we pick up a pen or type out a sentence, but to take on these conventions as if they are different shades of color in the artist's palette. The patterns of language are used to create, to say something new, to say what we need to say, to dream of what could be.

This book, this method of inviting students to look at conventions of language, is just a sliver of all the things your classroom is. But if this tiny sliver creates space for experimentation with language, creates space for authors of color to be celebrated, creates space where young learners feel the possibilities of what they can achieve as writers, then it has served its purpose.

And so it goes. As we continue to learn and grow—to read, to speak, to write, to make our voices heard—we'll continue finding our power and our students' power in two languages.

Sigan soñando,
Caroline

Into the Lessons

2

What Do Capital Letters Do?

¿Cuál es la función de las letras mayúsculas?

hildren know the difference between capital and lower case letters, but they don't always know why or how to use either with intention. One of the main goals of the lessons included in this chapter is to help writers understand that capital letters are used for a purpose. We only use capitals for a reason.

Students will need several focus phrases to meet specific capitalization goals. Like the capital cities in each state of our nation, capital letters are used to signify importance and emphasis. And when capitalization is used haphazardly, emphasis is lost and confusion reigns.

As author's craft, capitalization makes a word stand out to a reader, which reveals something about it. In addition to shaping our sentences, capital letters show that proper nouns or names are being used rather than common nouns.

Lesson Sets:

2.1 Las letras mayúsculas en los nombres de personas

2.2 Las letras mayúsculas en los títulos

2.3 Las letras mayúsculas en el saludo y en la despedida de una carta

2.4 Las letras mayúsculas en épocas históricas

Correlating English lessons for this chapter can be found in *Patterns of Power,* Chapter 4.

2.1 Las letras mayúsculas en los nombres de personas

Estándar Los nombres propios de personas se escriben con letra inicial mayúscula.

Frase de enfoque Uso letras mayúsculas al inicio de los nombres y apellidos de personas.

Invitación a notar Ella le enseña mi pintura a doña Andasola quien se la muestra a Gabino, su canario.
—Juan Felipe Herrera, *El niño de cabeza/The Upside Down Boy*

Power Note *Students might also notice the use of an irregular verb* (muestra) *and that names of pets* (Gabino) *are capitalized as well. Some students might note the appositive in this sentence as the phrase* su canario *is set off by a comma. In Spanish, the appositive is known as* la aposición explicativa *when one noun describes the noun that precedes it. In this case, the reader understands that* Gabino *is the name of the pet canary.*

Invitación a comparar Ella le enseña mi pintura a doña Andasola quien se la muestra a Gabino, su canario.

Él le enseñó mi tarea a la Sra. Gómez quien se la mostró al Sr. Rodríguez, el director.

Power Note *When you ask students to identify how the two sentences are alike or different, they may note the difference between* doña *and* Sra. *Discuss with students that, in Spanish, titles for people are capitalized when they are abbreviated but not when they are written out.*

Invitación a imitar *Imitate Together:* Invite students to write a sentence with you, using interactive writing.

> Mi amigo le enseña mi libro nuevo a Pablo quien se la muestra a la Sra. Márquez, la bibliotecaria.

Imitate Independently: Students use the model sentences and the sentences created by the class to compose their own sentences, capitalizing names and titles as appropriate.

Invitación a celebrar *After students orally share their sentences with the class, make a chart with the focus phrase at the top. Under the focus phrase, collect the capitalized names students are finding in their reading and writing, including the sentences they have created. When creating the chart in Spanish, create a separate section for names of places, as they will not follow the same pattern as first and last names of people (examples:* el parque Zilker *or* la escuela primaria Hillcrest*).*

Invitación a aplicar

Respond to Reading: Students write about a character from read-aloud, shared or independent reading time. They make sure to capitalize the names of the characters or people.

Invitación a corregir

¿Qué aprendimos de Juan Felipe Herrera acerca de la escritura?	
Ella le enseña mi pintura a doña Andasola quien se la muestra a Gabino, su canario.	
¿Qué ha cambiado? ¿Cuál es el efecto del cambio?	
(A) Ella le enseña mi pintura a doña andasola quien se la muestra a Gabino, su canario.	Andasola *empieza con una letra minúscula. Cuando no usamos una letra mayúscula en los apellidos, no puede ser un apellido según el patrón de "Uso las letras mayúsculas en los nombres y apellidos."*
(B) Ella le enseña mi pintura a Doña Andasola quien se la muestra a Gabino, su canario.	Doña *empieza con una letra mayúscula. En español, los títulos de las personas no llevan mayúscula cuando están escritos de forma completa.*
(C) Ella le enseña mi pintura a doña Andasola quien se la muestra a gabino, su canario.	Gabino *empieza con letra minúscula. Sabemos que hasta los nombres de las mascotas llevan mayúscula inicial.*

Figure 2.1a
First graders working on their imitations

Figure 2.1b
A first grader shares her sentence

¿Qué notas?

Ella le enseña mi pintura a doña Andasola quien se la muestra a Gabino, su canario.

—Juan Felipe Herrera, *El niño de cabeza/The Upside Down Boy*

¿En qué se parecen? ¿En qué se diferencian?

Ella le enseña mi pintura a doña Andasola quien se la muestra a Gabino, su canario.

Él le enseñó mi tarea a la Sra. Gómez quien se la mostró al Sr. Rodríguez, el director.

Inténtalo

Ella le enseña mi pintura a doña Andasola quien se la muestra a Gabino, su canario.

Él le enseñó mi tarea a la Sra. Gómez quien se la mostró al Sr. Rodríguez, el director.

Ella le enseña mi pintura a doña Andasola quien se la muestra a Gabino, su canario.

¿Qué ha cambiado? ¿Cuál es el efecto del cambio?

(A) Ella le enseña mi pintura a doña andasola quien se la muestra a Gabino, su canario.

(B) Ella le enseña mi pintura a Doña Andasola quien se la muestra a Gabino, su canario.

(C) Ella le enseña mi pintura a doña Andasola quien se la muestra a gabino, su canario.

2.2 Las letras mayúsculas en los títulos

Estándar Se escribe con mayúscula la primera palabra de los títulos de libros o películas.

Frase de enfoque Uso una letra mayúscula al principio de un título.

Invitación a notar Cristina quiere ser escritora cuando sea grande. Está escribiendo un libro de aventuras titulado *Cuentos de unicornios.*
—Saraí González y Monica Brown, *Saraí salva la música*

Power Note *As students share their noticings about these sentences, ask them what they know for sure about capitalizing titles. For bilingual students, you should draw students' attention to the differences in the patterns for capitalizing titles in the two languages.*

Invitación a comparar Cristina quiere ser escritora cuando sea grande. Está escribiendo un libro de aventuras titulado *Cuentos de unicornios.*

Jacqueline Woodson es la autora de un libro titulado *El día en que descubres quién eres.*

Power Note *Because we can't italicize when we write by hand, we can underline the titles. If your students are ready to discuss when we might capitalize words in a title other than the first word, consider using this sentence as a third sentence:*

Monica Brown escribió un libro llamado Mariposas en la calle Carmen.

Discuss with students why we find another capital letter. Carmen *refers to the street name and, therefore, is a proper noun.*

Invitación a imitar *Imitate Together:* Invite writers to use interactive or shared writing to compose a sentence with you using a movie, book, or TV show title.

Imitate Independently: Students use the model to create their own sentences, capitalizing the first word of the titles of written works or movies.

Invitación a celebrar Start a collection of titles under the focus phrase *Uso una letra mayúscula al principio de un título.*

Figure 2.2
First graders begin collaboratively creating a chart of capitalization patterns in book titles

Yo puedo usar letras mayusculas en los titulos.
Otto se Presenta Para Presidente
ELEPHANTS
ELEFANTES
¡ES un libr!
HOMBRE PERRO SE DESATA
La Vida del Perro
La Vida del Pingüino
Los colores
Nancy la elegante
El espacio
El mejor nido
¡Qué bien es ser yo mismo!
La Paloma y la Luna
Huevos verdes con Jamón
Que PaSa Cuanbo LLueve

Invitación a aplicar

Write a sentence answering the question: *¿Cuál es tu libro, película o programa de televisión favorito?* Put student responses together, perhaps in a class book. If it's written by hand, underline titles. If it's written on the computer, italicize titles. Don't do both.

Invitación a corregir

¿Qué aprendimos de Saraí González y Monica Brown acerca de la escritura?	
Cristina quiere ser escritora cuando sea grande. Está escribiendo un libro de aventuras titulado *Cuentos de unicornios.*	
¿Qué ha cambiado? ¿Cuál es el efecto del cambio?	
(A) Cristina quiere ser escritora cuando sea grande. Está escribiendo un libro de aventuras titulado *Cuentos de Unicornios.*	Unicornios *tiene una letra mayúscula inicial. Esto sigue el patrón del inglés. Sin embargo, en español solamente usamos letra mayúscula en la primera palabra.*
(B) Cristina quiere ser escritora cuando sea grande. Está escribiendo un libro de aventuras titulado cuentos de unicornios.	*No hay ninguna indicación en esta oración que* Cuentos de unicornios es *un título. Faltan la letra mayúscula al inicio y las letras itálicas.*
(C) Cristina quiere ser escritora cuando sea grande. Está escribiendo un Libro de aventuras titulado *Cuentos de unicornios.*	Libro es *un sustantivo común y no necesita mayúscula. Tampoco es parte del título.*

¿Qué notas?

Cristina quiere ser escritora cuando sea grande. Está escribiendo un libro de aventuras titulado *Cuentos de unicornios*.

—Saraí González y Monica Brown, Saraí salva la música

¿En qué se parecen? ¿En qué se diferencian?

Cristina quiere ser escritora cuando sea grande. Está escribiendo un libro de aventuras titulado *Cuentos de unicornios*.

Jacqueline Woodson es la autora de un libro titulado *El día en que descubres quién eres*.

Inténtalo

Cristina quiere ser escritora cuando sea grande. Está escribiendo un libro de aventuras titulado *Cuentos de unicornios.*

Jacqueline Woodson es la autora de un libro titulado *El día en que descubres quién eres.*

Cristina quiere ser escritora cuando sea grande. Está escribiendo un libro de aventuras titulado *Cuentos de unicornios.*

¿Qué ha cambiado? ¿Cuál es el efecto del cambio?

(A) Cristina quiere ser escritora cuando sea grande. Está escribiendo un libro de aventuras titulado *Cuentos de Unicornios.*

(B) Cristina quiere ser escritora cuando sea grande. Está escribiendo un libro de aventuras titulado cuentos de unicornios.

(C) Cristina quiere ser escritora cuando sea grande. Está escribiendo un Libro de aventuras titulado *Cuentos de unicornios.*

2.3 Las letras mayúsculas en el saludo y en la despedida de una carta

Estándar Los saludos y las despedidas de una carta se escriben con letra inicial mayúscula.

Frase de enfoque Uso la letra mayúscula al inicio del saludo y de la despedida de una carta.

Invitación a notar Mi querida familia:

He estado pizcando uvas y fresas en los campos de Delano, a 140 millas al norte de Los Ángeles, ahorrando dinero y pensando todo el tiempo en ustedes. Es un trabajo muy duro, que cansa mucho. Aquí en los campos hay un hombre que se llama César Chávez y que habla de uniones, huelgas y boicots. Estas nuevas palabras nos dan la esperanza de mejorar las condiciones de nosotros los que trabajamos en las fincas.

Hasta ahora, ha sido difícil conseguir las tarjetas verdes, pues no somos nosotros la única familia que trata de comenzar una nueva vida aquí. Por favor, tengan paciencia. No pasará mucho tiempo hasta que podamos estar todos juntos otra vez.

Abrazos y besitos,
Papá
—Amada Irma Pérez, *Mi diario de aquí hasta allá*

Figure 2.3a
Focus Phrase and the Invitation to Notice in a first-grade classroom. The teacher supports language development for students learning Spanish in a dual language classroom by drawing grapes and a strawberry.

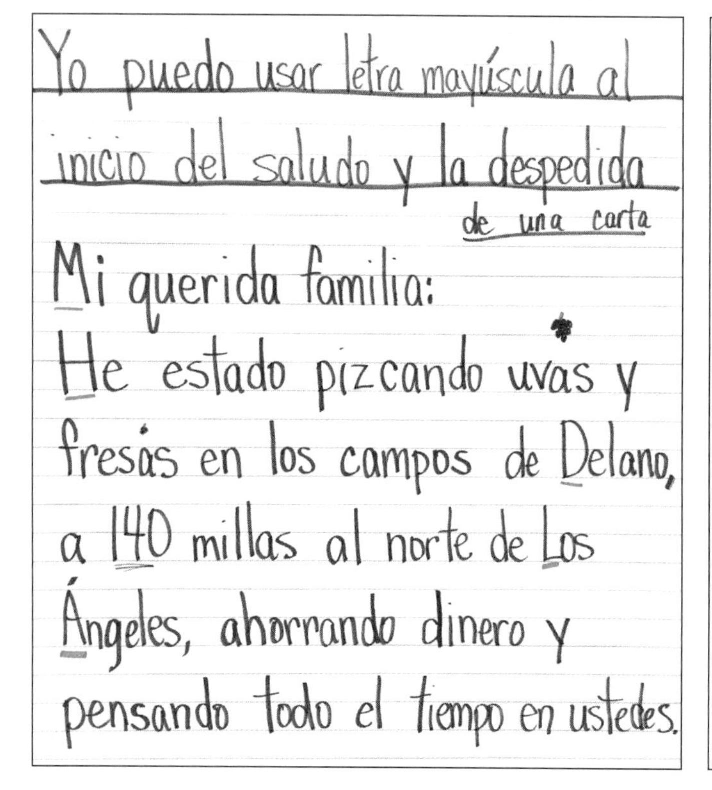

Power Note *Our focus in this example is on the opening and closing of the letter* (el saludo y la despedida). *Students will likely notice other attributes of the letter (capitalized names of people and places, a comma to separate items in a list, or compound sentences). Acknowledge what they notice, but also guide them to focus on the opening or the closing of the letter:* Uso la letra mayúscula al inicio del saludo y de la despedida de una carta.

Invitación a comparar

Mi querida familia:

He estado pizcando uvas y fresas en los campos de Delano, a 140 millas al norte de Los Ángeles, ahorrando dinero y pensando todo el tiempo en ustedes. Es un trabajo muy duro, que cansa mucho. Aquí en los campos hay un hombre que se llama César Chávez y que habla de uniones, huelgas y boicots. Estas nuevas palabras nos dan la esperanza de mejorar las condiciones de nosotros los que trabajamos en las fincas.

Hasta ahora, ha sido difícil conseguir las tarjetas verdes, pues no somos nosotros la única familia que trata de comenzar una nueva vida aquí. Por favor, tengan paciencia. No pasará mucho tiempo hasta que podamos estar todos juntos otra vez.

Abrazos y besitos,
Papá
—Amada Irma Pérez, *Mi diario de aquí hasta allá*

Querida tía Norma:

He estado trabajando mucho en la escuela, intentando a mejorar mis calificaciones para estar en la lista de honor. Es un trabajo muy duro, pero lo puedo lograr. Aquí en la escuela hay una maestra que me motiva mucho. Sus palabras me dan la esperanza de que puedo alcanzar mi meta de sacar buenas calificaciones.

Hasta ahora ha sido un poco difícil. No pasará mucho tiempo para que te escriba nuevamente enviándote mi reporte de progreso de la escuela.

Tu sobrina,
Ana

Power Note *Students will likely notice that the* N *in* Norma *is also capitalized in this comparison. If this confuses them, take some time to discuss how this letter opening has two capitalization patterns in it—opening letters and proper nouns.*

Invitación a imitar

Imitate Together: Invite writers to use interactive, shared, or paired writing to compose a letter with you.

Imitate Independently: Students use the model to create their own letters capitalizing the first word in the opening and closing, as well as names.

Invitación a celebrar

Share the letters aloud and have students mail or hand deliver their letters to the people they wrote them to if appropriate. This celebration might also include how to address an envelope.

Invitación a aplicar

Develop a list of ways authors open and close a letter. Have students write a letter to their favorite author, choosing the best way to open and close it. Mail the letters to the authors. They might even respond!

Invitación a corregir

¿Qué aprendimos de Amada Irma Pérez acerca de la escritura?	
Por favor, tengan paciencia. No pasará mucho tiempo hasta que podamos estar todos juntos otra vez. Abrazos y besitos, Papá	
¿Qué ha cambiado? ¿Cuál es el efecto del cambio?	
(A) Abrazos y Besitos, Papá	Besitos *tiene una letra mayúscula, aunque no es la primera palabra. Debido a que solo usamos una letra mayúscula al principio de la despedida, el lector quizás pensaría que no estaba escrita con mucho cuidado.*
(B) Abrazos, y besitos Papá	*Hay una coma después de abrazos. Esta coma dice al lector que tome una pausa en medio de la despedida. Solamente una coma es necesaria al final de la frase de la despedida.*
(C) Abrazos Y Besitos, Papá	*Cuando usamos letras mayúsculas en cada palabra, las palabras como los nombres propios que necesitan letras mayúsculas pierden su importancia. Solamente la primera palabra en una despedida requiere una letra mayúscula.*

Figure 2.3b
Second graders write their own letters

¿Qué notas?

Mi querida familia:

He estado pizcando uvas y fresas en los campos de Delano, a 140 millas al norte de Los Ángeles, ahorrando dinero y pensando todo el tiempo en ustedes. Es un trabajo muy duro, que cansa mucho. Aquí en los campos hay un hombre que se llama César Chávez y que habla de uniones, huelgas y boicots. Estas nuevas palabras nos dan la esperanza de mejorar las condiciones de nosotros los que trabajamos en las fincas.

Hasta ahora, ha sido difícil conseguir las tarjetas verdes, pues no somos nosotros la única familia que trata de comenzar una nueva vida aquí. Por favor, tengan paciencia. No pasará mucho tiempo hasta que podamos estar todos juntos otra vez.

Abrazos y besitos,
Papá
—Amada Irma Pérez, *Mi diario de aquí hasta allá*

¿En qué se parecen? ¿En qué se diferencian?

Mi querida familia:

He estado pizcando uvas y fresas en los campos de Delano, a 140 millas al norte de Los Ángeles, ahorrando dinero y pensando todo el tiempo en ustedes. Es un trabajo muy duro, que cansa mucho. Aquí en los campos hay un hombre que se llama César Chávez y que habla de uniones, huelgas y boicots. Estas nuevas palabras nos dan la esperanza de mejorar las condiciones de nosotros los que trabajamos en las fincas.

Hasta ahora, ha sido difícil conseguir las tarjetas verdes, pues no somos nosotros la única familia que trata de comenzar una nueva vida aquí. Por favor, tengan paciencia. No pasará mucho tiempo hasta que podamos estar todos juntos otra vez.

Abrazos y besitos,
Papá
—Amada Irma Pérez, *Mi diario de aquí hasta allá*

Querida tía Norma:

He estado trabajando mucho en la escuela, intentando mejorar mis calificaciones para estar en la lista de honor. Es un trabajo muy duro, pero lo puedo lograr. Aquí en la escuela hay una maestra que me motiva mucho. Sus palabras me dan la esperanza de que puedo alcanzar mi meta de sacar buenas calificaciones.

Hasta ahora ha sido un poco difícil. No pasará mucho tiempo para que te escriba nuevamente enviándote mi reporte de progreso de la escuela.

Tu sobrina,
Ana

Inténtalo

Mi querida familia:

He estado pizcando uvas y fresas en los campos de Delano, a 140 millas al norte de Los Ángeles, ahorrando dinero y pensando todo el tiempo en ustedes. Es un trabajo muy duro, que cansa mucho. Aquí en los campos hay un hombre que se llama César Chávez y que habla de uniones, huelgas y boicots. Estas nuevas palabras nos dan la esperanza de mejorar las condiciones de nosotros los que trabajamos en las fincas.

Hasta ahora, ha sido difícil conseguir las tarjetas verdes, pues no somos nosotros la única familia que trata de comenzar una nueva vida aquí. Por favor, tengan paciencia. No pasará mucho tiempo hasta que podamos estar todos juntos otra vez.

Abrazos y besitos,
Papá

—Amada Irma Pérez, *Mi diario de aquí hasta allá*

Por favor, tengan paciencia. No pasará mucho tiempo hasta que podamos estar todos juntos otra vez.

Abrazos y besitos,
Papá

¿Qué ha cambiado? ¿Cuál es el efecto del cambio?

(A) Abrazos y Besitos,
Papá

(B) Abrazos, y besitos
Papá

(C) Abrazos Y Besitos,
Papá

2.4 Las letras mayúsculas en épocas históricas

Estándar Las épocas históricas y los acontecimientos históricos se escriben con letras mayúsculas.

Frase de enfoque Uso las letras mayúsculas para enfatizar la importancia de las épocas históricas y los acontecimientos históricos.

Invitación a notar Cuando Dolores era niña, se mudó a California con su mamá y sus hermanos. Allí se hizo miembro de las Girl Scouts y ayudó a recaudar dinero para los soldados que luchaban en la Segunda Guerra Mundial.
—Monica Brown, *Lado a lado: La historia de Dolores Huerta y César Chávez*

Power Note *A note to the bilingual educator: decades are not capitalized in Spanish as they are in English (*The Nineties=los [años] noventa*). The article that precedes the historic period or document is not capitalized (*el Renacimiento*). When working with bilingual students, it's important to note the differences in languages.*

Invitación a comparar Cuando Dolores era niña, se mudó a California con su mamá y sus hermanos. Allí se hizo miembro de las Girl Scouts y ayudó a recaudar dinero para los soldados que luchaban en la Segunda Guerra Mundial.

Cuando César era joven, su familia perdió su casa durante la Gran Depresión. Se salió de estudiar en el séptimo grado y decidió ingresar a la Marina de los Estados Unidos.

Power Note *Students may note the capital letters in* California *and* los Estados Unidos. *The phrase* la Marina de los Estados Unidos *refers to an organization (U.S. Navy) and should be capitalized.*

Invitación a imitar *Shared Writing:* As a class compose a sentence using one of the historical periods listed on the chart. Students will try this out with a partner in the *Invitation to Apply.*

Invitación a aplicar Partners should choose a historical period from the chart and complete a quick internet search to gather enough information to write a few sentences about the time period on an index card. Writers make sure they use capital letters when writing about historical periods.

El uso de las letras mayúsculas en los acontecimientos históricos		
la Edad de Piedra la Edad Media la Edad de los Metales	el Renacimiento la Revolución francesa la Primera Guerra Mundial	la Gran Depresión la Segunda Guerra Mundial la Guerra de Vietnam

Invitación a celebrar

Share oral presentations of what students discovered. Reports could follow the relative time order in which they occurred, and the index cards could be taped to butcher paper creating an actual timeline.

Invitación a corregir

¿Qué aprendimos de Monica Brown acerca de la escritura?	
Cuando Dolores era niña, se mudó a California con su mamá y sus hermanos. Allí se hizo miembro de las Girl Scouts y ayudó a recaudar dinero para los soldados que luchaban en la Segunda Guerra Mundial.	
¿Qué ha cambiado? ¿Cuál es el efecto del cambio?	
(A) Cuando Dolores era niña, se mudó a california con su mamá y sus hermanos. Allí se hizo miembro de las Girl Scouts y ayudó a recaudar dinero para los soldados que luchaban en la Segunda Guerra Mundial.	California *no empieza con una letra mayúscula. Cuando no usamos una letra mayúscula, no estamos honrando al lugar o siguiendo el patrón. Usamos letras mayúsculas para los nombres de los lugares específicos.*
(B) Cuando Dolores era niña, se mudó a California con su mamá y sus hermanos. Allí se hizo miembro de las Girl Scouts y ayudó a recaudar dinero para los soldados que luchaban en la segunda guerra mundial.	La Segunda Guerra Mundial *se debe escribir con letras mayúsculas. Cuando no usamos letras mayúsculas, no enfatizamos la importancia del suceso. Usamos letras mayúsculas para los sucesos históricos.*
(C) Cuando Dolores era niña, se mudó a California con su mamá y sus hermanos. Allí se hizo miembro de las girl scouts y ayudó a recaudar dinero para los soldados que luchaban en la Segunda Guerra Mundial.	Las Girl Scouts es *una organización específica y se debe escribir con letras mayúsculas. Usamos letras mayúsculas para escribir el nombre de una organización o club.*

¿Qué notas?

Cuando Dolores era niña, se mudó a California con su mamá y sus hermanos. Allí se hizo miembro de las Girl Scouts y ayudó a recaudar dinero para los soldados que luchaban en la Segunda Guerra Mundial.

—*Monica Brown, Lado a lado: La historia de Dolores Huerta y César Chávez*

¿En qué se parecen? ¿En qué se diferencian?

Cuando Dolores era niña, se mudó a California con su mamá y sus hermanos. Allí se hizo miembro de las Girl Scouts y ayudó a recaudar dinero para los soldados que luchaban en la Segunda Guerra Mundial.

Cuando César era joven, su familia perdió su casa durante la Gran Depresión. Se salió de estudiar en el séptimo grado y decidió ingresar a la Marina de los Estados Unidos.

Inténtalo

Cuando Dolores era niña, se mudó a California con su mamá y sus hermanos. Allí se hizo miembro de las Girl Scouts y ayudó a recaudar dinero para los soldados que luchaban en la Segunda Guerra Mundial.

Cuando César era joven, su familia perdió su casa durante la Gran Depresión. Se salió de estudiar en el séptimo grado y decidió ingresar a la Marina de los Estados Unidos.

Cuando Dolores era niña, se mudó a California con su mamá y sus hermanos. Allí se hizo miembro de las Girl Scouts y ayudó a recaudar dinero para los soldados que luchaban en la Segunda Guerra Mundial.

¿Qué ha cambiado? ¿Cuál es el efecto del cambio?

(A) Cuando Dolores era niña, se mudó a california con su mamá y sus hermanos. Allí se hizo miembro de las Girl Scouts y ayudó a recaudar dinero para los soldados que luchaban en la Segunda Guerra Mundial.

(B) Cuando Dolores era niña, se mudó a California con su mamá y sus hermanos. Allí se hizo miembro de las Girl Scouts y ayudó a recaudar dinero para los soldados que luchaban en la segunda guerra mundial.

(C) Cuando Dolores era niña, se mudó a California con su mamá y sus hermanos. Allí se hizo miembro de las girl scouts y ayudó a recaudar dinero para los soldados que luchaban en la Segunda Guerra Mundial.

3

What Do Nouns Do?

¿Cuál es la función de los sustantivos?

Nouns are the stuff that things are made of. In fact, the world we live in is made of nouns. Where are you sitting or lying right now? In a chair? On a couch? In a bed? All the places where we could be are nouns. Sentences need stuff—or nouns—to be about something. The essential stuff of a basic sentence is referred to as its subject—the *who* or *what* of the sentence. We ask, "Who or what does or is something?" To identify the subject easily. The subject—or noun—will be the answer. Of course nouns do more than act as subjects of sentences. Writers use nouns all over their sentences to show a clear picture of people, places, and things.

And the more specific our nouns, the more concrete our writing becomes. The word *thing* doesn't give the mind a specific picture. The common noun *bug* does. Choosing a specific bug such as a *roach* gives us an even clearer picture. And when authors want to sharpen images by using names, they use proper nouns, capitalizing them to make sure they get the attention they deserve.

Lesson Sets:

3.1 Los sustantivos

3.2 Los nombres propios de personas y lugaress

3.3 Cuándo se usa la letra mayúscula y cuándo no

3.4 El plural de los sustantivos

3.5 Los sustantivos colectivos

3.6 La acentuación en los sustantivos

Correlating English lessons for this chapter can be found in *Patterns of Power*, Chapter 5.

3.1 Los sustantivos

Estándar Usar y entender los sustantivos comunes.

Frase de enfoque Uso los sustantivos para crear una imagen de personas, lugares y cosas.

Invitación a notar Con una pluma y un tintero un artista puede pintar al mundo entero.
—Alma Flor Ada, *Caballete*

Power Note *The nouns in this sentence are* pluma, tintero, artista *and* mundo. *Review with students that nouns* (sustantivos) *express people, places, things, or ideas. Encourage students to visualize the nouns in the sentence and how they support mental images.*

Invitación a comparar Con una pluma y un tintero un artista puede pintar al mundo entero.

Con un lápiz y un cuaderno un niño se convierte en autor.

Power Note *Help students notice the nouns in this imitation and discuss what they do. If your students are ready, ask which noun serves as the subject of the sentence. Students may also notice the pattern of beginning with a prepositional phrase.*

Invitación a imitar *Imitate Together:* Invite writers to use interactive or shared writing to compose a sentence with you.

Imitate Independently: Students use the model to create their own sentences, using nouns to help our reader understand the message.

Figure 3.1a
Focus phrase, Invitation to Notice, Invitation to Compare and Contrast, and Shared Writing in a first grade classroom

Uso los sustantivos para crear una imagen de personas, lugares y cosas.

Con una pluma y un tintero un artista puede pintar al mundo entero. —Alma Flor Ada, Caballete

Con un lápiz y un cuaderno un niño se convierte en autor.

La maestra y los niños salieron de la escuela y miraba un arco iris.

Figure 3.1b and 3.1c
Bilingual students work on their nouns in their writers notebooks

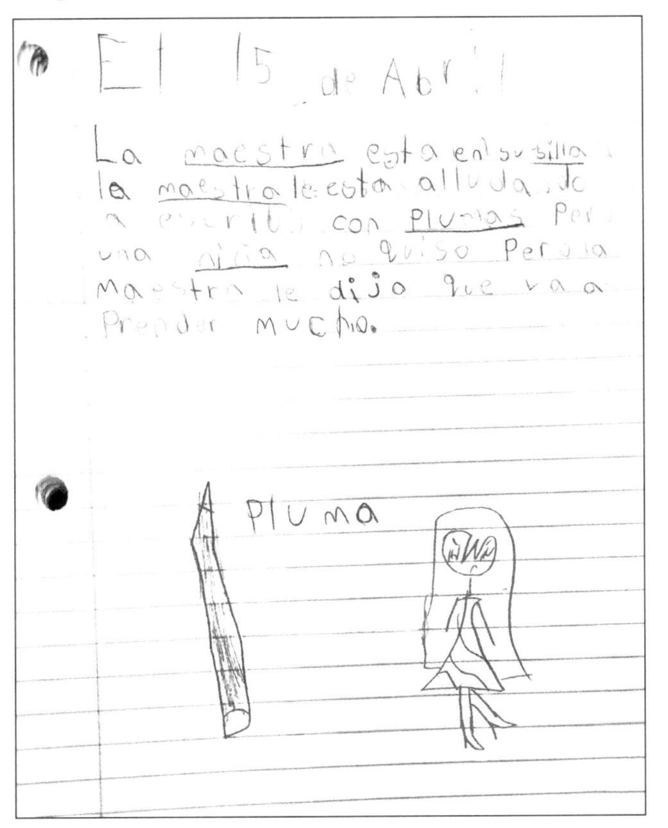

Invitación a celebrar

Open a new document on a class computer and write the focus phrase across the top: *Uso los sustantivos para crear una imagen de personas, lugares y cosas.* Throughout the day, students can take turns typing in their imitations. Make sure they put their name after an em dash on the line after their sentence like we do in all the lessons:

> *Con un controlador y una consola de videojuegos un niño se puede convertir en superheroe.*
> —Andrea

The next day, you can read and discuss the sentences as a class. Print the pages and distribut them to the class the day after that.

Invitación a aplicar

In another content-area, ask questions as the students find an interesting or favorite sentence:

- *¿Pueden decir* de quién *o* de qué *se trata?* Students can discuss with a neighbor.
- *¿Qué sustantivos crean una imagen más clara?* The class can continue the discussion and put their thinking on a chart.
- *Cuando escriban hoy, piensan en cómo van a usar los sustantivos específicos para crear una imagen para el lector.*

Invitación a corregir

¿Qué aprendimos de Alma Flor Ada acerca de la escritura?	
Con una pluma y un tintero un artista puede pintar al mundo entero.	
¿Qué ha cambiado? ¿Cuál es el efecto del cambio?	
(A) Con una pluma y un tintero un artista pueden pintar al mundo entero.	*El verbo* pueden *se usa con los sujetos plurales. Cuando los verbos y sujetos no concuerdan, es confuso para el lector.*
(B) Con una pluma y un tintero un artista puede pintar al mundo entera.	*El adjetivo* entera *debe describir al sustantivo* mundo. *Sin embargo,* mundo *es un sustantivo masculino y tenemos que usar* entero *para describirlo. Los adjetivos y sustantivos tienen que concordar.*
(C) Con la pluma y el tintero un artista puede pintar al mundo entero.	*Los artículos* la *y* el *indican una pluma y tintero específico.* Una *y* un *indican que pueden ser cualquier pluma o tintero.*

¿Qué notas?

Con una pluma y un tintero un artista puede pintar al mundo entero.

—Alma Flor Ada, *Caballete*

¿En qué se parecen? ¿En qué se diferencian?

Con una pluma y un tintero un artista puede pintar al mundo entero.

Con un lápiz y un cuaderno un niño se convierte en autor.

Inténtalo

Con una pluma y un tintero un artista puede pintar al mundo entero.

Con un lápiz y un cuaderno un niño se convierte en autor.

Con una pluma y un tintero un artista puede pintar al mundo entero.

¿Qué ha cambiado? ¿Cuál es el efecto del cambio?

(A) Con una pluma y un tintero un artista pueden pintar al mundo entero.

(B) Con una pluma y un tintero un artista puede pintar al mundo entera.

(C) Con la pluma y el tintero un artista puede pintar al mundo entero.

3.2 Los nombres propios de personas y lugares

Estándar Usar y entender los nombres propios.

Frase de enfoque Uso las letras mayúsculas en los nombres propios para enfatizar los nombres de personas y lugares específicos.

Invitación a notar En la cuarta tarde del verano, Octavio Rivera soñó cuatro puercos de Iowa que caían de una piñata y los puercos tenían alas amarillas y volaban hacia Chicago para visitar a su tío Glen y a su tía Nancy.
—Benjamín Alire Sáenz, *Un tiempo perfecto para soñar*

Power Note *Students may notice that this sentence contains three independent clauses. Discuss why they think the author chose to write one long sentence instead of breaking it up into two or three shorter sentences.*

Invitación a comparar En la cuarta tarde del verano, Octavio Rivera soñó cuatro puercos de Iowa que caían de una piñata y los puercos tenían alas amarillas y volaban hacia Chicago para visitar a su tío Glen y a su tía Nancy.

En la quinta tarde de verano, Octavio Rivera soñó cinco coyotes vestidos de mariachi que caían de una piñata y los coyotes se escapaban del Café Tencha en la calle Alameda y se dirigían a Denver en un tractor viejo y desbaratado.

Power Note *Use this sentence to review how street names are capitalized in Spanish.*

Invitación a imitar *Imitate Together:* Invite writers to used paired writing to compose a sentence.

Imitate Independently: Students use the model sentence to create their own sentences, using proper nouns to name specific people or places.

Invitación a celebrar At the top of a piece of chart paper, write the focus phrase. Add students' imitation sentences to the chart.

Invitación a aplicar Students return to a piece of writing—a writer's notebook entry, a draft, or a completed piece. Using the Rapid Revision/Revisión rápida technique (see Figure 3.2), they revise one or two sentences, changing common nouns to proper nouns.

Figure 3.2
Rapid Revision

Revisión rápida
- Releo mi escritura 2 veces.
- Busco en dónde puedo usar el patrón gramatical para expresar mejor mis ideas.
- Hago los cambios.
- Releo mi escritura para asegurar que tenga sentido.

Invitación a corregir

¿Qué aprendimos de Benjamín Alire Sáenz acerca de la escritura?	
En la cuarta tarde del verano, Octavio Rivera soñó cuatro puercos de Iowa que caían de una piñata y los puercos tenían alas amarillas y volaban hacia Chicago para visitar a su tío Glen y a su tía Nancy.	
¿Qué ha cambiado? ¿Cuál es el efecto del cambio?	
(A) En la cuarta tarde del verano, Octavio Rivera soñó cuatro puercos de iowa que caían de una piñata y los puercos tenían alas amarillas y volaban hacia chicago para visitar a su tío Glen y a su tía Nancy.	*Los nombres propios de lugares específicos no llevan letra mayúscula. Si no empezamos los nombres propios de lugares con una letra mayúscula, no estamos siguiendo el patrón de* Uso las letras mayúsculas en los nombre propios para enfatizar los nombres de personas y lugares específicos.
(B) En la cuarta tarde del verano, octavio rivera soñó cuatro puercos de Iowa que caían de una piñata y los puercos tenían alas amarillas y volaban hacia Chicago para visitar a su tío Glen y a su tía Nancy.	*Octavio Rivera está escrito con letras minúsculas. Usamos una letra mayúscula al principio de los nombres y apellidos de las personas.*
(C) En la cuarta tarde del verano, Octavio Rivera soñó cuatro puercos de Iowa que caían de una piñata y los puercos tenían alas amarillas y volaban hacia Chicago para visitar a su Tío Glen y a su Tía Nancy.	Tío *y* Tía *están escritos con una letra mayúscula. En este caso, el uso del pronombre posesivo* su *nos indica que* tío *y* tía *son sustantivos comunes y no son nombres propios.*

¿Qué notas?

En la cuarta tarde del verano, Octavio Rivera soñó cuatro puercos de Iowa que caían de una piñata y los puercos tenían alas amarillas y volaban hacia Chicago para visitar a su tío Glen y a su tía Nancy.
—Benjamín Alire Sáenz, *Un tiempo perfecto para soñar*

¿En qué se parecen? ¿En qué se diferencian?

En la cuarta tarde del verano, Octavio Rivera soñó cuatro puercos de Iowa que caían de una piñata y los puercos tenían alas amarillas y volaban hacia Chicago para visitar a su tío Glen y a su tía Nancy.

En la quinta tarde de verano, Octavio Rivera soñó cinco coyotes vestidos de mariachi que caían de una piñata y los coyotes se escapaban del Café Tencha en la calle Alameda y se dirigían a Denver en un tractor viejo y desbaratado.

Inténtalo

En la cuarta tarde del verano, Octavio Rivera soñó cuatro puercos de Iowa que caían de una piñata y los puercos tenían alas amarillas y volaban hacia Chicago para visitar a su tío Glen y a su tía Nancy.

En la quinta tarde de verano, Octavio Rivera soñó cinco coyotes vestidos de mariachi que caían de una piñata y los coyotes se escapaban del Café Tencha en la calle Alameda y se dirigían a Denver en un tractor viejo y desbaratad

En la cuarta tarde del verano, Octavio Rivera soñó cuatro puercos de Iowa que caían de una piñata y los puercos tenían alas amarillas y volaban hacia Chicago para visitar a su tío Glen y a su tía Nancy.

¿Qué ha cambiado? ¿Cuál es el efecto del cambio?

(A) En la cuarta tarde del verano, Octavio Rivera soñó cuatro puercos de iowa que caían de una piñata y los puercos tenían alas amarillas y volaban hacia chicago para visitar a su tío Glen y a su tía Nancy.

(B) En la cuarta tarde del verano, octavio rivera soñó cuatro puercos de Iowa que caían de una piñata y los puercos tenían alas amarillas y volaban hacia Chicago para visitar a su tío Glen y a su tía Nancy.

(C) En la cuarta tarde del verano, Octavio Rivera soñó cuatro puercos de Iowa que caían de una piñata y los puercos tenían alas amarillas y volaban hacia Chicago para visitar a su Tío Glen y a su Tía Nancy.

3.3 Cuándo se usa la letra mayúscula y cuándo no

Estándar Usar y entender los nombres propios.

Frase de enfoque Uso las letras mayúsculas en los nombres propios de personas, lugares o cosas.

Invitación a notar Mi nombre es Agua, pero todos me conocen por "Agüita".
—Jorge Tetl Argueta, *Agua, Agüita*

Power Note *Draw students' attention to the capital letters in* Agua *and* Agüita. *Ask them if they would normally put a capital letter for these words. Provide example sentences:* ¿Puedo tomar agua? Me bañé con agua caliente. *Ask students why these words are capitalized in the model sentence but not in the examples you have given.*

Invitación a comparar Mi nombre es Agua, pero todos me conocen por "Agüita".

Me llamo Ángel, pero no me porto como un ángel.

Power Note *In compound sentences in Spanish, a comma should be used before certain conjunctions. Find more on compound sentences in Chapter 13.*

Invitación a imitar *Imitate Together:* Invite writers to used paired writing to compose a sentence.

Imitate Independently: Students should use the model sentence to create their own sentences using proper nouns for specific names of places, people, or things.

Figure 3.3a
Focus Phrase, Invitation to Notice, Invitation to Imitate, and Shared Writing

Uso letras mayúsculas en los nombres propios de las personas, lugares o cosas.
Mi nombre es Agua, pero todos me conocen por "Agüita".
Me llamo Ángel; pero no me porto como un ángel.
Yo tengo una hermana que se llama Magdalena.

Invitación a celebrar

Create a wall chart with the focus phrase. Add sentences that students say, write, or find. Highlight the capitalization patterns.

Invitación a aplicar

Students return to a piece of writing from their notebooks, drafts, or a completed piece. Use the Rapid Revision technique described in Lesson 3.2, Figure 3.2. Students should find one or two instances where they can change common nouns to proper nouns.

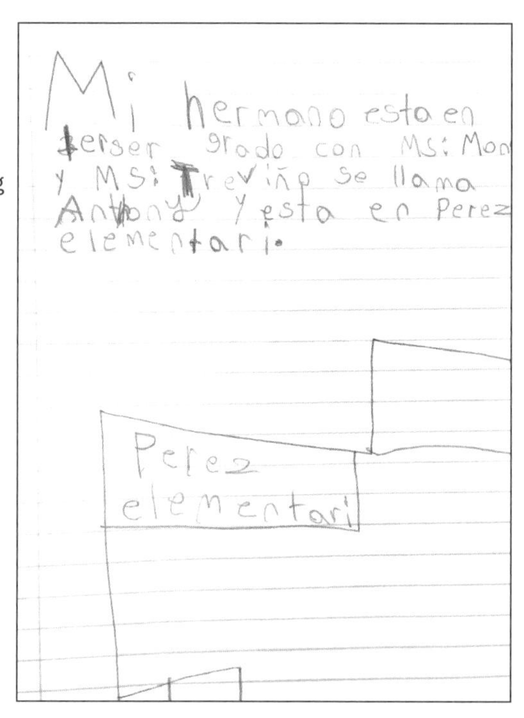

Figure 3.3b
A bilingual first grader thinks through capitalizing the first word of the sentence and names throughout. The student uses the English phrasing to name the school, but a Spanish spelling pattern. In Spanish we would write *la escuela primaria Pérez*. We celebrate the language knowledge that crosses over from one language to another and use these moments to teach the differences in English and Spanish.

Invitación a corregir

¿Qué aprendimos de Jorge Tetl Argueta acerca de la escritura?	
Mi nombre es Agua, pero todos me conocen por "Agüita".	
¿Qué ha cambiado? Cuál es el efecto del cambio?	
(A) Mi nombre es agua, pero todos me conocen por "agüita".	Agua y Agüita *aquí empiezan con letras minúsculas. Aunque normalmente las palabras* agua *y* agüita *no llevan letra mayúscula, sirven como nombres propios en esta oración.*
(B) Mi nombre es Agua y todos me conocen por "Agüita".	*La conjunción ha cambiado en esta oración. El significado de la oración cambia sutilmente. Aunque su nombre es Agua, le llaman Aguita. Como la gente no le dice por su nombre, la conjunción* pero *es mejor.*
(C) Mi nombre es Agua pero todos me conocen por "Agüita".	*No hay una coma antes de la conjunción* pero*. En español no es necesario usar una coma con la conjunción* y *en una oración compuesta. Sin embargo, una oración compuesta con la conjunción* pero *debe tener una coma.*

¿Qué notas?

Mi nombre es Agua, pero todos me conocen por "Agüita".
—Jorge Tetl Argueta, *Agua, Agüita*

¿En qué se parecen? ¿En qué se diferencian?

Mi nombre es Agua, pero todos me conocen por "Agüita".

Me llamo Ángel, pero no me porto como un ángel.

Inténtalo

Mi nombre es Agua, pero todos me conocen por "Agüita".

Me llamo Ángel, pero no me porto como un ángel.

Mi nombre es Agua, pero todos me conocen por "Agüita".

¿Qué ha cambiado? ¿Cuál es el efecto del cambio?

(A) Mi nombre es agua, pero todos me conocen por "agüita".

(B) Mi nombre es Agua y todos me conocen por "Agüita".

(C) Mi nombre es Agua pero todos me conocen por "Agüita".

3.4 El plural de los sustantivos

Estándar Usar y entender los sustantivos en forma singular y plural.

Frase de enfoque Uso los sustantivos plurales para mostrar más de una persona, lugar o cosa.

Invitación a notar Antes, mucho antes de que los españoles soñaron con llegar a estas tierras, tus antepasados, indios náhuas como tú, ya vivían aquí.
—Jorge Argueta, *Xochitl, la Niña de las Flores*

Power Note *You'll notice that to make the word* español *plural, writers add* -es. *The pattern in Spanish shows that words that end in* -d, -j, -l, -n *or* -r *need* –es *to make the plural form of the noun.*

Invitación a comparar Antes, mucho antes de que los españoles soñaron con llegar a estas tierras, tus antepasados, indios náhuas como tú, ya vivían aquí.

Antes, mucho antes de que construyeron los puentes en la frontera, tus abuelos, méxico-americanos como tú, caminaban libremente entre los dos países.

Power Note *Students may note that in both sentences ethnicities or nationalities are not capitalized in Spanish. For bilingual students, it is important to note that in English these types of words do need to be capitalized.*

Invitación a imitar *Imitate Together:* Invite writers to use interactive or shared writing to compose a sentence with you.

Imitate Independently: Students use the model to create their own sentences, using plural nouns.

Invitación a aplicar Students find a sentence in their reading or writing that uses a plural noun. Then they copy the sentence into their writer's notebook and write a few sentences explaining how they know what the plural noun is and what would change in the sentence if the noun were singular.

Invitación a corregir

¿Qué aprendimos de Jorge Argueta acerca de la escritura?	
Antes, mucho antes de que los españoles soñaron con llegar a estas tierras, tus antepasados, indios náhuas como tú, ya vivían aquí.	
¿Qué ha cambiado? ¿Cuál es el efecto del cambio?	
(A) Antes, mucho antes de que los españols soñaron con llegar a estas tierras, tus antepasados, indios náhuas como tú, ya vivían aquí.	*A* españoles *le falta la* e. *Según el patrón del español, los sustantivos que terminan con una consonante requieren -es al final de la palabra.*
(B) Antes, mucho antes de que los españoles soñaron con llegar a esta tierras, tus antepasados, indios náhuas como tú, ya vivían aquí.	*A la palabra* esta *le falta la* s. *Las palabras* estas tierras *tienen que concordar en cantidad.*
(C) Antes, mucho antes de que los Españoles soñaron con llegar a estas tierras, tus antepasados, indios náhuas como tú, ya vivían aquí.	*En español no se requiere una letra mayúscula inicial para nombrar las nacionalidades. Los españoles debe estar escrito en letra minúscula.*

Figure 3.4
Fourth graders collect their invitations on the board

¿Qué notas?

Antes, mucho antes de que los españoles soñaron con llegar a estas tierras, tus antepasados, indios náhuas como tú, ya vivían aquí.

—Jorge Argueta, *Xochitl, la Niña de las Flores*

¿En qué se parecen? ¿En qué se diferencian?

Antes, mucho antes de que los españoles soñaron con llegar a estas tierras, tus antepasados, indios náhuas como tú, ya vivían aquí.

Antes, mucho antes de que construyeron los puentes en la frontera, tus abuelos, méxico-americanos como tú, caminaban libremente entre los dos países.

Inténtalo

Antes, mucho antes de que los españoles soñaron con llegar a estas tierras, tus antepasados, indios náhuas como tú, ya vivían aquí.

Antes, mucho antes de que construyeron los puentes en la frontera, tus abuelos, méxico-americanos como tú, caminaban libremente entre los dos países.

Antes, mucho antes de que los españoles soñaron con llegar a estas tierras, tus antepasados, indios náhuas como tú, ya vivían aquí.

¿Qué ha cambiado? ¿Cuál es el efecto del cambio?

(A) Antes, mucho antes de que los españols soñaron con llegar a estas tierras, tus antepasados, indios náhuas como tú, ya vivían aquí.

(B) Antes, mucho antes de que los españoles soñaron con llegar a esta tierras, tus antepasados, indios náhuas como tú, ya vivían aquí.

(C) Antes, mucho antes de que los Españoles soñaron con llegar a estas tierras, tus antepasados, indios náhuas como tú, ya vivían aquí.

3.5 Los sustantivos colectivos

Estándar Usar y entender los sustantivos colectivos.

Frase de enfoque Uso los sustantivos colectivos para nombrar grupos de personas, lugares o cosas.

Invitación a notar Su padre criaba asnos para venderlos y ella cuidaba la manada mientras pastaba.
—Xavier Garza y Gabriela Baeza Ventura, *Kid Cyclone Fights the Devil and Other Stories*

Power Note *This is a great time to review compound sentences. The subjects and predicates of each part are clear. But the focus of this lesson should go to collective nouns. Students may not be sure what kind of animal* manada *refers to. We normally see* manada *associated with cows. In addition to noticing the collective noun* manada, *it's essential to notice the verb that goes with it. Ask students why they think the authors used* pastaba *instead of* pastaban.

Invitación a comparar Su padre criaba asnos para venderlos y ella cuidaba la manada mientras pastaba.

La gente piensa que soy presumida, pero realmente soy tímida y callada.

Power Note *In this imitation we look at different ways to combine sentences into one compound sentence by using conjunctions. Have students look for the word that indicates a group of something. Then look at the verb associated with it. If students are having trouble noticing that collective nouns use singular conjugations, compare the phrase* las personas piensan *and* la gente piensa. *The meaning doesn't change but the verb does.*

Invitación a imitar *Imitate Together:* Invite writers to use interactive or shared writing to compose a sentence with you.

Imitate Independently: Students use the model to create their own sentences, using collective noun. Co-creating a list of common collective nouns will help students get started.

Invitación a celebrar We continue adding to our collective noun chart as we find words in our reading, writing, or speaking.

Invitación a aplicar Highlight any collective nouns found in other subject areas. Discuss how the articles and verbs around them treat the collective noun as one entity (singular).

Invitación a corregir

¿Qué aprendimos de Xavier Garza y Gabriela Baeza Ventura acerca de la escritura?	
Su padre criaba asnos para venderlos y ella cuidaba la manada mientras pastaba.	
¿Qué ha cambiado? ¿Cuál es el efecto del cambio?	
(A) Su padre criaba asnos para venderlos y ella cuidaba las vacas mientras pastaba.	*Reemplazamos* manada *con* las vacas. *Aunque la idea es la misma, el verbo tiene que concordar con el sustantivo.* Las vacas *es una idea plural y requiere el verbo* pastaban.
(B) Su padre criaba asnos para venderlos pero ella cuidaba la manada mientras pastaba.	*La conjunción* pero *indica un contraste. Eso cambia el significado original de los autores. También, la conjunción requiere una coma antes para unir dos oraciones simples.*
(C) Su padre criaba asnos para venderlos. Ella cuidaba la manada mientras pastaba.	*Tenemos dos oraciones simples. Ahora parecen dos ideas separadas en vez de una idea de lo que hace cada uno.*

¿Qué notas?

Su padre criaba asnos para venderlos y ella cuidaba la manada mientras pastaba.

—Xavier Garza y Gabriela Baeza Ventura, *Kid Cyclone Fights the Devil and Other Stories*

¿En qué se parecen? ¿En qué se diferencian?

Su padre criaba asnos para venderlos y ella cuidaba la manada mientras pastaba.

La gente piensa que soy presumida, pero realmente soy tímida y callada.

Inténtalo

Su padre criaba asnos para venderlos y ella cuidaba la manada mientras pastaba.

La gente piensa que soy presumida, pero realmente soy tímida y callada.

Su padre criaba asnos para venderlos y ella cuidaba la manada mientras pastaba.

¿Qué ha cambiado? ¿Cuál es el efecto del cambio?

(A) Su padre criaba asnos para venderlos y ella cuidaba las vacas mientras pastaba.

(B) Su padre criaba asnos para venderlos pero ella cuidaba la manada mientras pastaba.

(C) Su padre criaba asnos para venderlos. Ella cuidaba la manada mientras pastaba.

3.6 La acentuación en los sustantivos

Estándar Usar los acentos ortográficos.

Frase de enfoque Uso los acentos ortográficos para denotar cómo se pronuncia una palabra.

Invitación a notar Le gustaba la idea de que México, el país donde su papá había nacido, fuera el primer país extranjero que visitara.
—Angela Cervantes, *Frida, el misterio del anillo del pavo real y yo*

Power Note *If students are not noticing the accented words, ask them if this sentence refers to a potato (papa) born in México or to a father (papá) born in México. Students will laugh, but ask them how they know the difference. Ask students where they find other accented words and what effect the accent has on the pronunciation of the word.*

Invitación a comparar Le gustaba la idea de que México, el país donde su papá había nacido, fuera el primer país extranjero que visitara.

Le encantaba la idea de que podía aprender la gramática leyendo una oración de algún libro.

Power Note *As students notice the accented words in this imitation, try pronouncing the words as if they had no accent. In general, the second to last syllable is accented in Spanish.*

Invitación a imitar *Imitate Together:* Invite writers to use interactive or shared writing to compose a sentence with you using common accented words (*papá, mamá, avión, río, él*, etc.).

> A mi mamá y mi papá les gustaba la idea de ir al zoológico para ver los pájaros y murciélagos.

Imitate Independently: Students use the models to compose their own sentences using more than one word that requires an accent.

Invitación a celebrar Students can share their imitations on a Padlet, class blog, wall chart, door chart, or hall chart.

Invitación a aplicar Students should return to a piece of writing and work with a peer to identify words they wrote with accents and words that might need an accent. Students should verify in a dictionary if the word uses an accent. Help students look out for words that lose their accent when they are written as plurals (example: león-leones).

Invitación a corregir

¿Qué aprendimos de Angela Cervantes acerca de la escritura?	
Le gustaba la idea de que México, el país donde su papá había nacido, fuera el primer país extranjero que visitara.	
¿Qué ha cambiado? ¿Cuál es el efecto del cambio?	
(A) Le gustaba la idea de que México, el país donde su papa había nacido, fuera el primer país extranjero que visitara.	*Papa (sin acento) es algo que podemos comer. Como estamos hablando del padre de la niña, usamos* papá *con el acento escrito.*
(B) Le gustaba la idea de que México, el pais donde su papá había nacido, fuera el primer pais extranjero que visitara.	*Cuando escribimos pais sin un acento escrito, se pronunica como la palabra* pies *en inglés. Para hablar de una nación, necesitamos usar un acento escrito en país.*
(C) Le gustaba la idea de que méxico, el país donde su papá había nacido, fuera el primer país extranjero que visitara.	*México empieza con letra minúscula. El nombre de un país debe llevar letra mayúscula al* inicio.

¿Qué notas?

Le gustaba la idea de que México, el país donde su papá había nacido, fuera el primer país extranjero que visitara.

—Angela Cervantes, *Frida, el misterio del anillo del pavo real y yo*

¿En qué se parecen? ¿En qué se diferencian?

Le gustaba la idea de que México, el país donde su papá había nacido, fuera el primer país extranjero que visitara.

Le encantaba la idea de que podía aprender la gramática leyendo una oración de algún libro.

Inténtalo

Le gustaba la idea de que México, el país donde su papá había nacido, fuera el primer país extranjero que visitara.

Le encantaba la idea de que podía aprender la gramática leyendo una oración de algún libro.

Le gustaba la idea de que México, el país donde su papá había nacido, fuera el primer país extranjero que visitara.

¿Qué ha cambiado? ¿Cuál es el efecto del cambio?

(A) Le gustaba la idea de que México, el país donde su papa había nacido, fuera el primer país extranjero que visitara.

(B) Le gustaba la idea de que México, el pais donde su papá había nacido, fuera el primer pais extranjero que visitara.

(C) Le gustaba la idea de que méxico, el país donde su papá había nacido, fuera el primer país extranjero que visitara.

4

What Do Verbs Do?

¿Cuál es la función de los verbos?

Sentences wouldn't *do* or *be* much without a workhorse verb.

Tom.

See? Nothing happens.

Tom cooks.

Verbs activate sentences, bringing them to life, identifying actions, setting a mood or telling time. Quite simply, verbs help us *do* and *be*. And in addition to actions, verbs also signal a state of existence, linking nouns or pronouns to a description. *You are a magnificent writer*. They even help out other verbs from time to time.

Verbs can get tricky for many young writers when we get down to concepts like past, present and future tense as well as irregular verbs. But together, with conversation and practice, we can face it all with ease—one verb at a time.

Lesson Sets:

4.1 Los verbos demuestran acción

4.2 El verbo *ser*

4.3 El verbo *ser* (tiempo futuro)

4.4 Los tiempos verbales

4.5 Los verbos irregulares

4.6 Los acentos ortográficos en los verbos pretéritos

Correlating English lessons for this chapter can be found in *Patterns of Power*, Chapter 6.

4.1 Los verbos demuestran acción

Estándar Usar y entender la función de los verbos (acciones).

Frase de enfoque Uso los verbos para demostrar acciones.

Invitación a notar Llevo paletas para cantar y paletas para volar. Llevo paletas para bailar y paletas para soñar.
—Jorge Argueta, *Somos como las nubes*

Power Note *These sentences contain both conjungated* (llevo) *and infinitive verbs* (cantar, volar, bailar, *and* soñar). *Depending on the age of students you might make the distinction between the two types of verbs we find in this sentence, though all indicate an action. Students will love acting out the verbs in the sentence.*

Invitación a comparar Llevo paletas para cantar y paletas para volar. Llevo paletas para bailar y paletas para soñar.

Tengo libros para leer y libros para mirar. Tengo libros para aprender y libros para imaginar.

Power Note *In this imitation, the verbs* leer *and* mirar *are concrete actions. However,* aprender *and* imaginar *are more abstract. Discuss with students that actions don't always involve movement but that learning and imagining are still things we can do.*

Figure 4.1
A fourth grader plays with the pattern of the original sentence.

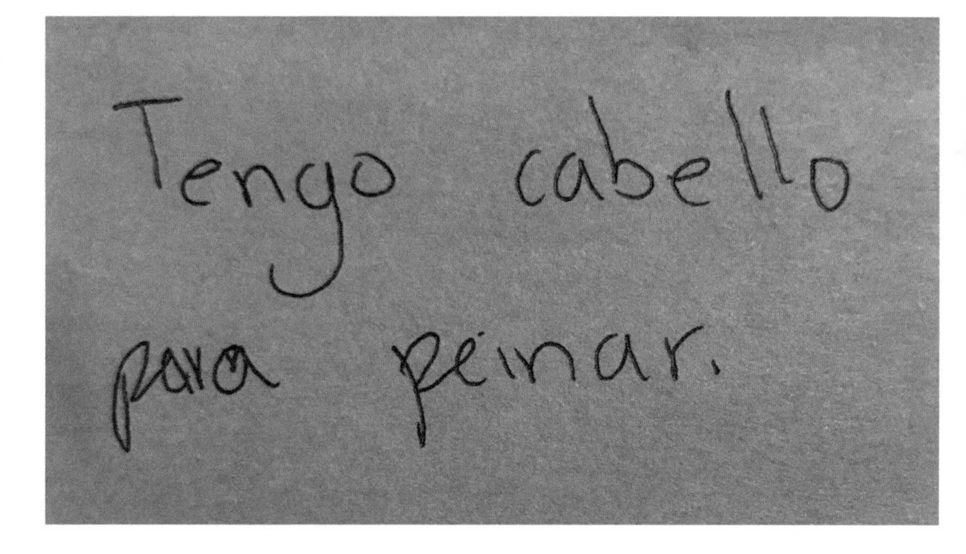

Invitación a imitar

Imitate Together: Partners should choose a noun to which they can apply various actions. Once they choose the subject of their sentences, they should think of actions that go with that subject. While working on their imitations, students should be able to see the previous invitations.

Imitate Independently: Students use the model sentences from the compare-and-contrast invitation as well as others created by the class to compose their own imitation.

Invitación a celebrar

Have students present in pairs. One should read the imitation sentence or sentences while the other acts out the movements.

Invitación a aplicar

In guided reading or after a read-aloud, review how verbs show what is happening in the text and will be part of any good summary. Invite writers to write a sentence about what is happening. Ask, "¿Necesitan usar los verbos para escribir acerca de este cuento? ¿Pueden describir qué está pasando en el texto sin usar los verbos? ¿Por qué?"

Invitación a corregir

¿Qué aprendimos de Jorge Argueta acerca de la escritura?	
Llevo paletas para cantar y paletas para volar. Llevo paletas para bailar y paletas para soñar.	
¿Qué ha cambiado? ¿Cuál es el efecto del cambio?	
(A) Llevé paletas para cantar y paletas para volar. Llevé paletas para bailar y paletas para soñar.	*Ahora* llevé *indica que este verbo está en el tiempo pretérito. Ya no es algo que ocurre en el presente. Los verbos infinitivos no cambiaron.*
(B) Llevo paletas para cantar y paletas para volar Llevo paletas para bailar y paletas para soñar.	*Se ha quitado el punto de la primera oración. Los puntos indican cuándo termina una oración. Cuando no usamos punto y seguido, se confunden los lectores.*
(C) Llevamos paletas para cantar y paletas para volar. Llevamos paletas para bailar y paletas para soñar.	*El verbo* llevo *se cambió a* llevamos *indicando que somos varios que están llevando paletas. En las oraciones originales, el narrador está hablando solamente de sí mismo.*

¿Qué notas?

Llevo paletas para cantar y paletas para volar. Llevo paletas para bailar y paletas para soñar.

—Jorge Argueta, *Somos como las nubes*

¿En qué se parecen? ¿En qué se diferencian?

Llevo paletas para cantar y paletas para volar. Llevo paletas para bailar y paletas para soñar.

Tengo libros para leer y libros para mirar. Tengo libros para aprender y libros para imaginar.

Inténtalo

Llevo paletas para cantar y paletas para volar. Llevo paletas para bailar y paletas para soñar.

Tengo libros para leer y libros para mirar. Tengo libros para aprender y libros para imaginar.

Llevo paletas para cantar y paletas para volar. Llevo paletas para bailar y paletas para soñar.

¿Qué ha cambiado? ¿Cuál es el efecto del cambio?

(A) Llevé paletas para cantar y paletas para volar. Llevé paletas para bailar y paletas para soñar.

(B) Llevo paletas para cantar y paletas para volar Llevo paletas para bailar y paletas para soñar.

(C) Llevamos paletas para cantar y paletas para volar. Llevamos paletas para bailar y paletas para soñar.

4.2 El verbo *ser*

Estándar Usar y entender los usos del verbo *ser* en el tiempo presente.

Frase de enfoque Uso las formas del verbo ser para indicar *qué es*.

Invitación a notar Las piedras son nuestros abuelos y abuelas.
—Jorge Argueta, "Las piedras" *de Hablando con Madre Tierra*

Power Note *Students often relate verbs to action words, but it is much harder for them to identify verbs like* ser. *Give students many examples of sentences with the conjugations of* ser *in the present tense* (soy, eres, es, somos, son). Mis estudiantes son inteligentes. Mi mamá es muy cariñosa. Somos escritores. *This will give them the opportunity to explore the verb* ser *in present tense.*

Invitación a comparar Las piedras son nuestros abuelos y abuelas.

La tierra es nuestra madre.

Power Note *Discuss with students why the verbs in these sentences are not the same. Ask students if* Las piedras es *sounds right. Students might then be able to explain that the verb* ser *changes depending on the subject.*

Invitación a imitar *Imitate Together:* Partners choose a subject (animal, person, or living thing). Once they have chosen it, the pair composes a sentence using *es* or *son*. Coach kids on how a singular or plural subject changes the verb.

Invitación a aplicar Begin a wall chart with all the ways we use the verb *ser*. Students can continue adding to the chart as they author more sentences or find them in their independent reading.

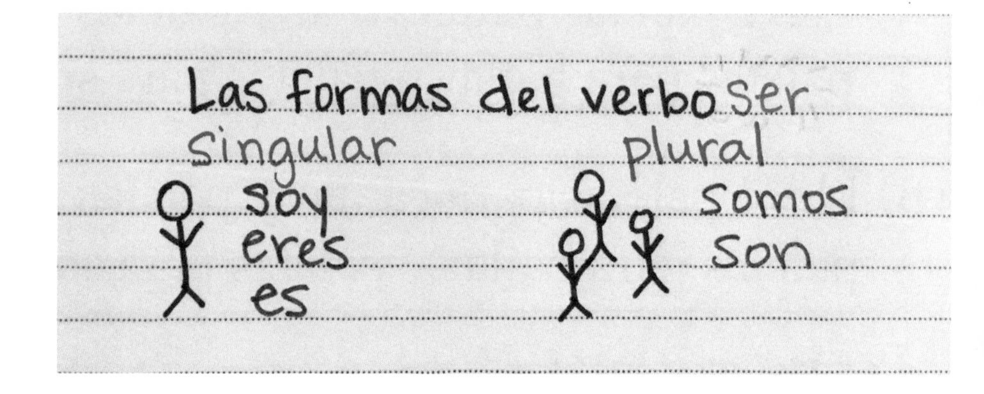

Figure 4.2
Conjugation chart for the present tense

Invitación a corregir

¿Qué aprendimos de Jorge Argueta acerca de la escritura?	
Las piedras son nuestros abuelos y abuelas.	
¿Qué ha cambiado? ¿Cuál es el efecto del cambio?	
(A) Las piedras es nuestros abuelos y abuelas.	*El sujeto* las piedras *no concuerda con el verbo. Tiene que haber concordancia entre los sujetos y los verbos.*
(B) La piedra son nuestros abuelos y abuelas.	*Este sujeto cambió de plural a singular. Un sujeto singular requiere el verbo es.*
(C) Las Piedras son nuestros abuelos y abuelas.	*El sustantivo común* piedras *no requiere una letra mayúscula. Cuando usamos una letra mayúscula fuera de lugar, el lector se puede confundir pensando que es un nombre propio.*

¿Qué notas?

Las piedras son nuestros abuelos y abuelas.
—Jorge Argueta, "Las piedras" de *Hablando con Madre Tierra*

¿En qué se parecen? ¿En qué se diferencian?

Las piedras son nuestros abuelos y abuelas.

La tierra es nuestra madre.

Inténtalo

Las piedras son nuestros abuelos y abuelas.

La tierra es nuestra madre.

Las piedras son nuestros abuelos y abuelas.

¿Qué ha cambiado? ¿Cuál es el efecto del cambio?

(A) Las piedras es nuestros abuelos y abuelas.

(B) La piedra son nuestros abuelos y abuelas.

(C) Las Piedras son nuestros abuelos y abuelas.

4.3 El verbo *ser* (tiempo futuro)

Estándar Usar y entender los usos del verbo *ser* en sus varias conjugaciones.

Frase de enfoque Uso el verbo *ser* en varias formas.

Invitación a notar ¿Seré yo la única que tiene miedo de dejar nuestro hogar, nuestra hermosa patria y toda la gente que quizás nunca más volvamos a ver?
—Amada Irma Pérez, *Mi diario de aquí hasta allá*

Power Note *Students may notice that* seré *is in future tense, though they may not be able to name the tense. Give students many examples of sentences with the conjugations of* ser *in the future and past tenses and invite them to discuss the differences they notice.*

Invitación a comparar ¿Seré yo la única que tiene miedo de dejar nuestro hogar, nuestra hermosa patria y toda la gente que quizás nunca más volvamos a ver?

¿Seré yo la unica que está ansiosa y tímida en el primer día de la escuela?

Power Note *As a possible extension, change the subject of the question.* ¿_____ ella la única que tiene miedo de dejar su hogar, su hermosa patria y toda la gente que quizás nunca más vuelva a ver?

Invitación a imitar *Imitate Together:* Invite students to use shared or interactive writing to compose a sentence with you.

> ¿Somos nosotros los únicos niños a los que les encanta el estudio de la gramática?

Imitate in Pairs: Generate with students a chart of all the ways they can think of to use the verb *ser*. Pairs can choose from the chart to create their sentences.

Invitación a celebrar Pairs will share their sentences aloud. Consider using Bomba Estereo's song "Soy yo" as an example of how we use *ser*.

Invitación a aplicar Have students look for examples of how the verb *ser* is used in their independent reading. Add examples to a chart of all the forms of *ser*.

Invitación a corregir

¿Qué aprendimos de Amada Irma Pérez acerca de la escritura?	
¿Seré yo la única que tiene miedo de dejar nuestro hogar, nuestra hermosa patria y toda la gente que quizás nunca más volvamos a ver?	
¿Qué ha cambiado? ¿Cuál es el efecto del cambio?	
(A) Seré yo la única que tiene miedo de dejar nuestro hogar, nuestra hermosa patria y toda la gente que quizás nunca más volvamos a ver.	*Los signos de interrogación han cambiado a un punto. En este ejemplo la narradora está diciendo algo en vez de preguntar algo.*
(B) ¿Serás yo la única que tiene miedo de dejar nuestro hogar, nuestra hermosa patria y toda la gente que quizás nunca más volvamos a ver?	*La palabra* serás *no concuerda con el sujeto* yo. *Los verbos y sujetos tienen que concordar.*
(C) ¿Fui yo la única que tiene miedo de dejar nuestro hogar, nuestra hermosa patria y toda la gente que quizás nunca más volvamos a ver?	*La palabra* fui *indica el pasado. En este ejemplo, parece que la narradora está preguntado sobre algo que ya pasó.*

¿Qué notas?

¿Seré yo la única que tiene miedo de dejar nuestro hogar, nuestra hermosa patria y toda la gente que quizás nunca más volvamos a ver?

—Amada Irma Pérez, *Mi diario de aquí hasta allá*

¿En qué se parecen? ¿En qué se diferencian?

¿Seré yo la única que tiene miedo de dejar nuestro hogar, nuestra hermosa patria y toda la gente que quizás nunca más volvamos a ver?

¿Seré yo la única que está ansiosa y tímida en el primer día de la escuela?

Inténtalo

¿Seré yo la única que tiene miedo de dejar nuestro hogar, nuestra hermosa patria y toda la gente que quizás nunca más volvamos a ver?

¿Seré yo la única que está ansiosa y tímida en el primer día de la escuela?

¿Seré yo la única que tiene miedo de dejar nuestro hogar, nuestra hermosa patria y toda la gente que quizás nunca más volvamos a ver?

¿Qué ha cambiado? ¿Cuál es el efecto del cambio?

(A) Seré yo la única que tiene miedo de dejar nuestro hogar, nuestra hermosa patria y toda la gente que quizás nunca más volvamos a ver.

(B) ¿Serás yo la única que tiene miedo de dejar nuestro hogar, nuestra hermosa patria y toda la gente que quizás nunca más volvamos a ver?

(C) ¿Fui yo la única que tiene miedo de dejar nuestro hogar, nuestra hermosa patria y toda la gente que quizás nunca más volvamos a ver?

4.4 Los tiempos verbales

Estándar Usar y entender los tiempos verbales para indicar cuándo ocurrió algo.

Frase de enfoque Uso los tiempos de los verbos para mostrar cuándo pasó algo.

Invitación a notar En la noche, mientras dormíamos, la piñata del cumpleaños se cayó del árbol como fruta demasiado madura y tiró todos los dulces.
—Jennifer Clement, el poema "Piñata" del *The Tree is Older Than You Are: A Bilingual Gathering of Poems & Stories from México with Paintings by Mexican Artists*

La piñata del cumpleaños se cae del árbol como fruta demasiado madura y tira todos los dulces.

La piñata del cumpleaños se caerá del árbol como fruta demasiado madura y tirará todos los dulces.

Power Note *In this invitation to notice we display three sentences in three tenses to draw attention to the effect of the different conjugations of the verbs. Discuss with students how the sentences are alike and different. Emphasize how verbs tell when an action took place or will take place.*

Invitación a comparar En la noche, mientras dormíamos, la piñata del cumplaños se cayó del árbol como fruta demasiado madura y tiró todos los dulces.

En la noche, el mapache tiró el bote de la basura y se comió el viejo pastel de cumpleaños.

Power Note *Ask students, "¿Los tiempos verbales son iguales? ¿Cómo sáben?" Experiment with changing the tenses of the verbs in the imitation sentence to help students note how verbs indicate time.*

Figure 4.4a
Focus Phrase and examples of different tenses

Uso el tiempo de los verbos para mostrar cuando algo pasó.

Pasado (ya pasó)
La piñata del cumpleaños se cayó del árbol como fruta demasiado madura y tiró todos los dulces.

Presente (ahora)
La piñata del cumpleaños se cae del árbol como fruta demasiado madura y tira todos los dulces.

Futuro (va a pasar)
La piñata del cumpleaños se caerá del árbol como fruta demasiado madura y tirará todos los dulces.

Invitación a imitar

Imitate Together: As a class, identify the tense of the original sentence. Together craft a sentence with a series of three actions in which the verbs use the same tense.

Imitate Independently: Students use the model sentence to craft their own, choosing a tense and using it consistently throughout.

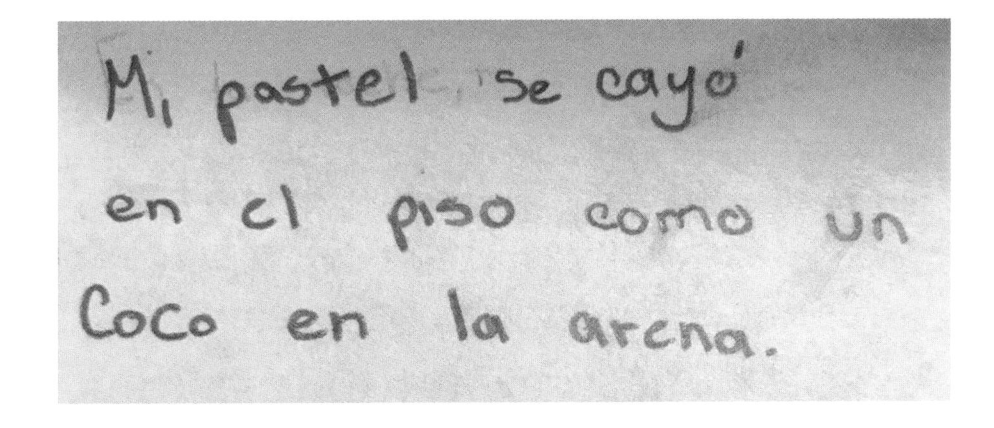

Figure 4.4b
A student uses verbs to show past tense while experimenting with figurative language

Invitación a aplicar

Students select a sentence from their independent reading. They identify the sentence's verb tense in the author's sentence. They then write two more versions of the sentences using verb tenses the author did not choose. Students should discuss the effect of the tense changes on the sentence.

Invitación a corregir

¿Qué aprendimos de Jennifer Clement acerca de la escritura?	
En la noche, mientras dormíamos, la piñata del cumpleaños se cayó del árbol como fruta demasiado madura y tiró todos los dulces.	
¿Qué ha cambiado? ¿Cuál es el efecto del cambio?	
(A) En la noche, mientras dormimos, la piñata del cumpleaños se cae del árbol como fruta demasiado madura y tiró todos los dulces.	*Los tiempos verbales no concuerdan en esta oración.* Tiró *indica el pasado, mientras* se cae *indica el presente. El verbo* dormimos *puede indicar el presente o el pasado.*
(B) En la noche, mientras dormíamos, la Piñata del Cumpleaños se cayó del árbol como fruta demasiado madura y tiró todos los dulces.	La piñata del cumpleaños *no es un nombre propio, así que no requiere letras mayúsculas al inicio de las palabras.*
(C) En la noche, mientras dormíamos, la piñata del cumpleaños se cayeron del árbol como fruta demasiado madura y tiraron todos los dulces.	*Los tiempos verbales en esta oración indican el pasado, pero no concuerdan con el sujeto.* Tiraron *y* se cayeron *indican sujetos plurales.*

¿Qué notas?

En la noche, mientras dormíamos, la piñata del cumpleaños se cayó del árbol como fruta demasiado madura y tiró todos los dulces.

—Jennifer Clement, el poema "Piñata" del *The Tree is Older Than You Are: A Bilingual Gathering of Poems & Stories from México with Paintings by Mexican Artists*

La piñata del cumpleaños se cae del árbol como fruta demasiado madura y tira todos los dulces.

La piñata del cumpleaños se caerá del árbol como fruta demasiado madura y tirará todos los dulces.

¿En qué se parecen? ¿En qué se diferencian?

En la noche, mientras dormíamos, la piñata del cumpleaños se cayó del árbol como fruta demasiado madura y tiró todos los dulces.

En la noche, el mapache tiró el bote de la basura y se comió el viejo pastel de cumpleaños.

Inténtalo

En la noche, mientras dormíamos, la piñata del cumplaños se cayó del árbol como fruta demasiado madura y tiró todos los dulces.

En la noche, el mapache tiró el bote de la basura y se comió el viejo pastel de cumpleaños.

En la noche, mientras dormíamos, la piñata del cumpleaños se cayó del árbol como fruta demasiado madura y tiró todos los dulces.

¿Qué ha cambiado? ¿Cuál es el efecto del cambio?

(A) En la noche, mientras dormimos, la piñata del cumpleaños se cae del árbol como fruta demasiado madura y tiró todos los dulces.

(B) En la noche, mientras dormíamos, la Piñata del Cumpleaños se cayó del árbol como fruta demasiado madura y tiró todos los dulces.

(C) En la noche, mientras dormíamos, la piñata del cumpleaños se cayeron del árbol como fruta demasiado madura y tiraron todos los dulces.

4.5 Los verbos irregulares

Estándar Usar y entender los verbos irregulares.

Frase de enfoque Aseguro que los verbos suenan bien.

Invitación a notar Habrá veces en que el almuerzo que te prepare tu mamá sea tan raro o tan desconocido para otros que no puedan entender lo mucho que a ti te gusta.
—Jacqueline Woodson, *El día en que descubres quién eres*

Power Note *There are so many verbs in this invitation! Take it in chunks. Students may be able to say that* habrá *is a verb but might not be able to say that it comes from the verb* haber*. Review with students that* hay *also comes from* haber*. Begin a chart titled* Verbos irregulares *(see example in Figure 4.5). Consider writing the infintive form in a bubble and webbing from it the versions that you find together. Other irregular verbs in this sentence include* sea *and* puedan*. The verb* entender *is irregular in some of its conjugations (ex.* entiendo*).*

Invitación a comparar Habrá veces en que el almuerzo que te prepare tu mamá sea tan raro o tan desconocido para otros que no puedan entender lo mucho que a ti te gusta.

Habrá veces en que el mundo te parezca un lugar en el que te encuentras completamente fuera de él.

Power Note *This imitation sentence comes from the same book by Jacqueline Woodson.* Parezca *and* encuentras *are irregular verbs in these conjugations and can be added to your irregular verbs chart.*

Figure 4.5
A class collection of irregular verbs from literature

Invitación a imitar

Imitate Together: After you've collected a few common irregular verbs, have students choose a verb from your chart (e.g., *poner, ir, ver, querer, ser, tener, pedir, poder, dar, hacer, saber, decir, venir,* etc.) and compose a sentence with you that uses at least one irregular verb.

Imitate Independently: Students use the model to create their own sentence, using an irregular verb.

Invitación a celebrar

Using sentences from their invitation to imitate or their writing notebook, create a chart of *verbos regulares y verbos irregulares*. From the sentences students share, categorize the verbs as regular or irregular. Ask students what patterns they notice.

Invitación a aplicar

Have students form two lines. One person from each line comes up to the front of the class. The teacher reads one verb from the list of irregular verbs. Whoever is able to use the verb in a sentence the most creatively and still make sense wins.

Invitación a corregir

¿Qué aprendimos de Jacqueline Woodson acerca de la escritura?	
Habrá veces en que el almuerzo que te prepare tu mamá sea tan raro o tan desconocido para otros que no puedan entender lo mucho que a ti te gusta.	
¿Qué ha cambiado? ¿Cuál es el efecto del cambio?	
(A) Haberá veces en que el almuerzo que te prepare tu mamá sea tan raro o tan desconocido para otros que no puedan entender lo mucho que a ti te gusta.	*El tiempo futuro de la palabra* habrá *cambió a* haberá. *Aunque sigue el patrón de los verbos en el tiempo futuro,* haberá *no es una palabra.*
(B) Habrá veces en que el almuerzo que te prepare tu mamá era tan raro o tan desconocido para otros que no puedan entender lo mucho que a ti te gusta.	*El verbo era no concuerda con el tiempo de los demás verbos. Es confuso para el lector si el tiempo de los verbos cambia dentro de una oración.*
(C) Habrá veces en que el almuerzo que te prepare tu mamá sea tan raro o tan desconocido para otros que no podan entender lo mucho que a ti te gusta.	*La conjugación del verbo* poder *no tiene sentido aquí.* Podan *no es una palabra e interfiere con el mensaje de la autora.*

¿Qué notas?

Habrá veces en que el almuerzo que te prepare tu mamá sea tan raro o tan desconocido para otros que no puedan entender lo mucho que a ti te gusta.

—Jacqueline Woodson, *El día en que descubres quién eres*

¿En qué se parecen? ¿En qué se diferencian?

Habrá veces en que el almuerzo que te prepare tu mamá sea tan raro o tan desconocido para otros que no puedan entender lo mucho que a ti te gusta.

Habrá veces en que el mundo te parezca un lugar en el que te encuentras completamente fuera de él.

Inténtalo

Habrá veces en que el almuerzo que te prepare tu mamá sea tan raro o tan desconocido para otros que no puedan entender lo mucho que a ti te gusta.

Habrá veces en que el mundo te parezca un lugar en el que te encuentras completamente fuera de él.

Habrá veces en que el almuerzo que te prepare tu mamá sea tan raro o tan desconocido para otros que no puedan entender lo mucho que a ti te gusta.

¿Qué ha cambiado? ¿Cuál es el efecto del cambio?

(A) Haberá veces en que el almuerzo que te prepare tu mamá sea tan raro o tan desconocido para otros que no puedan entender lo mucho que a ti te gusta.

(B) Habrá veces en que el almuerzo que te prepare tu mamá era tan raro o tan desconocido para otros que no puedan entender lo mucho que a ti te gusta.

(C) Habrá veces en que el almuerzo que te prepare tu mamá sea tan raro o tan desconocido para otros que no podan entender lo mucho que a ti te gusta.

4.6 Los acentos ortográficos en los verbos pretéritos

Estándar Los verbos en el tiempo del pretérito indefinido se escriben con acentos ortográficos en la primera y tercera persona del singular.

Frase de enfoque Uso el acento escrito en los verbos en el pasado.

Invitación a notar Mamá se sentó conmigo en el asiento de atrás del coche y me contó un cuento.
—René Colato Laínez, *Del Norte al Sur*

Power Note *Remind students that, in Spanish, we generally accent the second to last syllable when we pronounce words. To understand the function of the accent, pronounce the words as if they were not accented. Students will immediately recognize that, without the accent, the pronounciation results in nonsense words.*

Invitación a comparar Mamá se sentó conmigo en el asiento de atrás del coche y me contó un cuento.

Me senté con ella en la banca y le conté toda la historia.

Power Note *The imitation sentence uses a first person perspective. If students do not notice the difference of first and third person points-of-view, ask "Are the verbs the same?" As students note that both forms are accented, ask students how the verb would change if the subject was* tú, nosotros, ustedes *or* ellos.

Invitación a imitar *Imitate in Pairs:* The first student should write a sentence stating what they did yesterday. The second student should repeat that sentence in third person. Then, they should switch roles. Here is an example:

> Ayer comí fideos y terminé mi tarea temprano.
>
> Ayer comió fideos y terminó su tarea temprano.

Invitación a celebrar Have each student share aloud their sentence stating what they did yesterday. The class should respond orally with the same sentence in third person.

Invitación a aplicar Writers can return to a piece of writing in which they have written about a past experience. They should look for verbs that might require an accent.

Invitación a corregir

¿Qué aprendimos de René Colato Laínez acerca de la escritura?	
Mamá se sentó conmigo en el asiento de atrás del coche y me contó un cuento.	
¿Qué ha cambiado? ¿Cuál es el efecto del cambio?	
(A) Mamá se sento conmigo en el asiento de atrás del coche y me conto un cuento.	Sento *y* conto *no son palabras en español cuando no están escritas con el tilde. Para demostrar el tiempo pasado, usamos los tildes en la última sílaba.*
(B) Mamá se sienta conmigo en el asiento de atrás del coche y me cuenta un cuento.	*Los verbos han cambiado al tiempo presente. Eso cambia el significado de la oración que está sucediendo en este momento.*
(C) Mama se sentó conmigo en el asiento de atrás del coche y me contó un cuento.	Mama *está escrita sin el tilde en la última sílaba. Cuando está escrito así, la pronunciaríamos como la palabra en inglés.*

Figure 4.6
Students refer to a previous lesson to see how past-tense verbs were written.

¿Qué notas?

Mamá se sentó conmigo en el asiento de atrás del coche y me contó un cuento.

—René Colato Laínez, *Del Norte al Sur*

¿En qué se parecen? ¿En qué se diferencian?

Mamá se sentó conmigo en el asiento de atrás del coche y me contó un cuento.

Me senté con ella en la banca y le conté toda la historia.

Inténtalo

Mamá se sentó conmigo en el asiento de atrás del coche y me contó un cuento.

Me senté con ella en la banca y le conté toda la historia.

Mamá se sentó conmigo en el asiento de atrás del coche y me contó un cuento.

¿Qué ha cambiado? ¿Cuál es el efecto del cambio?

(A) Mamá se sento conmigo en el asiento de atrás del coche y me conto un cuento.

(B) Mamá se sienta conmigo en el asiento de atrás del coche y me cuenta un cuento.

(C) Mama se sentó conmigo en el asiento de atrás del coche y me contó un cuento.

5

What Do End Marks Do?

¿Cuál es la función de los puntos, los signos de interrogación y los signos de admiración?

Sentences aren't sentences without periods, question marks, or exclamation points. With the stroke of the pen or the tap of a key on our keyboard, writers direct how sentences are read. Do you want your sentences to make some noise or show some excitement? Use exclamation points. If you'd like your sentences to ask a question, use question marks. And, if you're merely stating something without fanfare, just the facts, conclude with a period. Just three marks total to learn, with only three jobs to do.

When writers take care with their end marks, they not only enhance sentence boundaries but also tell you if a sentence is a statement, question or exclamation. They orchestrate how we read the sentences that unfurl before us, one after the other.

Lesson Sets:

5.1 Mi voz y la puntuación

5.2 Los signos de interrogación

5.3 Los signos de admiración

5.4 Termino mis oraciones: Punto y seguido

Correlating English lessons for this chapter can be found in *Patterns of Power*, Chapter 8.

5.1 Mi voz y la puntuación

As we begin investigating the role of end punctuation, we focus on oral language. We forego our regular routine in this lesson to focus on noticing what punctuation does when we read out loud. When studying end punctuation, students need to experience how punctuation adds voice and rhythm to writing. Choral reading can build this understanding. Begin by displaying this excerpt from *Los remedios de mi tata* by Roni Capin Rivera-Ashford.

Power Note *When studying end punctuation, students need to experience how punctuation adds voice and rhythm to writing. Choral reading can build this understanding. Begin by displaying this excerpt from* Los remedios de mi tata *by Roni Capin Rivera-Ashford.*

- *Read the excerpt together with the teacher's voice guiding the reading.*
- *Read it again with an emphasis on what the punctuation tells us to do with our voices. Discuss what each mark tells us.*
- *Choose two or three lines to highlight and read them again with the focus on how punctuation changes your voice.*
- *Read the entire excerpt again.*

Students may read only the bold sentences.

Tu tata —dice Mamá—, siempre tiene un remedio, aunque simplemente sea un abrazo que te hace sentir mejor. Una vez yo le estaba ayudando a tu nana a picar lechuga para las chimichangas y me corté un dedo. Tu tata me puso el dedo a remojar en un líquido que hizo con Oshá o también le dicen Chuchupate. **Después, ¿sabes lo que hizo? ¡Metió mi dedo en un poco de café recién molido! El café llenó la herida y la cortada dejó de sangrar.**

5.2 Los signos de interrogación

Estándar Usar los signos de interrogación para formar preguntas.

Frase de enfoque Uso los signos de interrogación para formar preguntas.

Invitación a notar ¿Cómo les explico al mis padres que mi abuela quiere un tatuaje?
—Carlos Aguasaco, "Nueva en Nueva York" en *Cool Salsa*

Invitación a comparar ¿Cómo les explico al mis padres que mi abuela quiere un tatuaje?

¿Cómo cambia tu voz al leer una pregunta?

Power Note *Bilingual students might note the difference between punctuating questions in English and punctuating questions in Spanish. Remind them of the patterns for punctuating exclamatory sentences as well.*

Invitación a imitar *Imitate Together:* Invite writers to compose a sentence with you, using shared or interactive writing.

Invitación a celebrar *Punctuation Theater:* Students should perform their questions in pairs, making sure their inflection matches the question.

Invitación a aplicar While students read independently, invite them to look for questions they find in their reading. Discuss with students where they are finding questions (dialogue, character's thinking, question to the reader, etc.)

Invitación a corregir

¿Qué aprendimos de Carlos Aguasaco acerca de la escritura?	
¿Cómo les explico a mis padres que mi abuela quiere un tatuaje?	
¿Qué ha cambiado? ¿Cuál es el efecto del cambio?	
(A) Cómo les explico a mis padres que mi abuela quiere un tatuaje?	*No aparece el signo de interrogación al principio de la oración. Según el patrón del español, se requieren signos de interrogación al principio y al final de una pregunta.*
(B) Cómo les explico a mis padres que mi abuela quiere un tatuaje.	*Sin los signos de interrogación, el lector no sabe qué hacer con su voz al leer la oración en voz alta.*
(C) ¿Como les explico a mis padres que mi abuela quiere un tatuaje?	*A la palabra* como *le falta la tilde. Las palabras que se usan al principio de una pregunta llevan tilde (*qué, cuál, quién, cómo, cuán, cuánto, cuándo, dónde *y* adónde*).*

¿Qué notas?

¿Cómo les explico a mis padres que mi abuela quiere un tatuaje?

—Carlos Aguasaco, "Nueva en Nueva York" en *Cool Salsa*

¿En qué se parecen? ¿En qué se diferencian?

¿Cómo les explico a mis padres que mi abuela quiere un tatuaje?

¿Cómo cambia tu voz al leer una pregunta?

Inténtalo

¿Como les explico a mis padres que mi abuela quiere un tatuaje?

¿Cómo cambia tu voz al leer una pregunta?

¿Cómo les explico a mis padres que mi abuela quiere un tatuaje?

¿Qué ha cambiado? ¿Cuál es el efecto del cambio?

(A) Cómo les explico a mis padres que mi abuela quiere un tatuaje?

(B) Cómo les explico a mis padres que mi abuela quiere un tatuaje.

(C) ¿Como les explico a mis padres que mi abuela
quiere
un tatuaje?

5.3 Los signos de admiración

Estándar Usar los signos de admiración para indicar asombro.

Frase de enfoque Uso los signos de admiración para indicar asombro.

Invitación a notar Diego pintaba día y noche. ¡Sus amigos tenían que subir por una escalera para verlo!
—Jeanette y Jonah Winter, *Diego*

Invitación a comparar Diego pintaba día y noche. ¡Sus amigos tenían que subir por una escalera para verlo!

Frida pintó 200 obras de arte. ¡Más de 50 eran autorretratos!

Power Note *Compare patterns for punctuating exclamations in Spanish to patterns in English. Students will likely note that in Spanish we find punctuation at the beginning and end of the sentence.*

Invitación a imitar *Imitate Together:* Invite writers to compose a sentence with you, using interactive, shared, or paired writing.

Invitación a celebrar Students perform their sentences in pairs, exaggerating their exclamations!

Invitación a aplicar While students are reading, invite them to notice which end marks are used most often. Discuss with students which end mark they use most in their own writing as well. Look for patterns among certain types of sentences. Perhaps students will notice that questions often appear in dialogue or that exclamations are often short.

Invitación a corregir

¿Qué aprendimos de Jeanette y Jonah Winter acerca de la escritura?	
Diego pintaba día y noche. ¡Sus amigos tenían que subir por una escalera para verlo!	
¿Qué ha cambiado? ¿Cuál es el efecto del cambio?	
(A) Diego pintaba día y noche. Sus amigos tenían que subir por una escalera para verlo.	*No aparecen los signos de admiración en la segunda oración. Sin los signos, parece que es muy normal subir por una escalera para visitar a tus amigos.*
(B) Diego pintaba día y noche. Sus amigos tenían que subir por una escalera para verlo!	*Falta el signo de admiración al principio de la segunda oración. De esta manera, no sigue el patrón del español, sino el patrón del inglés.*
(C) ¡Diego pintaba día y noche! Sus amigos tenían que subir por una escalera para verlo.	*Al cambiar dónde colocamos los signos de admiración, cambia el sentido de asombro. Así, lo sorprendente es que pintaba todo el tiempo.*

¿Qué notas?

Diego pintaba día y noche. ¡Sus amigos tenían que subir por una escalera para verlo!
—Jeanette y Jonah Winter, *Diego*

¿En qué se parecen? ¿En qué se diferencian?

Diego pintaba día y noche. ¡Sus amigos tenían que subir por una escalera para verlo!
—Jeanette y Jonah Winter, *Diego*

Frida pintó 200 obras de arte. ¡Más de 50 eran autorretratos!

Inténtalo

Diego pintaba día y noche. ¡Sus amigos tenían que subir por una escalera para verlo!
—Jeanette y Jonah Winter, *Diego*

Frida pintó 200 obras de arte. ¡Más de 50 eran autorretratos!

Diego pintaba día y noche. ¡Sus amigos tenían que subir por una escalera para verlo!

¿Qué ha cambiado? ¿Cuál es el efecto del cambio?

(A) Diego pintaba día y noche. Sus amigos tenían que subir por una escalera para verlo.

(B) Diego pintaba día y noche. Sus amigos tenían que subir por una escalera para verlo!

(C) ¡Diego pintaba día y noche! Sus amigos tenían que subir por una escalera para verlo.

5.4 Termino mis oraciones: Punto y seguido

Estándar Usar el punto y seguido para pasar de una oración a otra.

Frase de enfoque Uso el punto y seguido para ayudar al lector a pasar de una oración a otra.

Invitación a notar Use the excerpt from *Los muchachos de la calle Ruiz* by Diane Gonzales Bertrand that is missing punctuation.

Power Note *Print and hand out the excerpt without punctuation from* Los muchachos de la calle Ruiz *by Diane Gonzales Bertand. The periods are missing and initial capital letters in sentences are lower case. Proper nouns are left with capital letters. Model using the first paragraph and saying, "I'll show you how." Read aloud the first paragraph, running ideas together as if it's written without periods. Ask students, "¿Hay ciertas partes en que les ayudaría a los lectores ver el punto y seguido?" You will mark the passage when the class agrees that there should be punctuation.*

Students continue working in pairs or groups of three to punctuate the rest of the passage. The groups or pairs then share their choices and their reasoning for inserting punctuation. The next day compare and contrast them with Gonzales Bertrand's version.

Invitación a comparar Use the excerpt from *Los muchachos de la calle Ruiz* by Diane Gonzales Bertrand that includes all punctuation. Ask students, *¿En qué se parecen? ¿En qué se diferencian?*

Power Note *Groups should compare and contrast their version to the author's version. Have them discuss their choices versus Gonzales Bertrand's choices. In this lesson, we forego our regular editing task since students have just worked intensely to edit an entire page of text. Celebrate all their efforts, even when they don't closely resemble the author's original writing. They are doing what writers do and thinking about where to break up ideas into sentences.*

¿Qué notas?

ese mismo día por la tarde finalmente vi a David con mis propios ojos mi hermana mis hermanos y yo caminábamos a casa de la panadería miré boquiabierto al muchacho que nos tapó el paso con su bici

su cabello corto me recordaba al viejo cepillo que Mamá usaba para limpiar pero este cepillo parecía haber tallado ladrillos rojos todo el día el muchacho tenía labios gruesos y una nariz ancha y plana parecía un triángulo al revés porque sus hombros eran anchos y su cuerpo era delgado su piel café estaba bien quemada por el sol

David se sentó en la bici de largo asiento rojo y cuadro blanco sucio parecía que se la había robado de una chatarrería llevaba una camiseta cuyas mangas habían sido cortadas y unos pantalones de mezclilla bien gastados que habían sido cortados justo debajo de las rodillas no llevaba calcetines dentro de sus sucios tenis de básquetbol

gran parte del peso de David se balanceaba en una pierna mientras estaba estacionando en la callejón entre la panadería y la florería todavía nos faltaba una cuadra para llegar a casa

ponte detrás de mí Joe dijo Mike y me jaló detrás de él
yo tenía ocho años y jamás me movía tan rápido como mis hermanos querían

mi hermano mayor Gabe se paró al lado de Mike nuestra hermana tina se acercó formaron una pared entre David y yo

¿En qué se parecen? ¿En qué se diferencian?

Ese mismo día por la tarde finalmente vi a David con mis propios ojos. Mi hermana, mis hermanos y yo caminábamos a casa de la panadería. Miré boquiabierto al muchacho que nos tapó el paso con su bici.

Su cabello corto me recordaba al viejo cepillo que Mamá usaba para limpiar, pero este cepillo parecía haber tallado ladrillos rojos todo el día. El muchacho tenía labios gruesos y una nariz ancha y plana. Parecía un triángulo al revés porque sus hombros eran anchos y su cuerpo era delgado. Su piel café estaba bien quemada por el sol.

David se sentó en la bici de largo asiento rojo y cuadro blanco sucio. Parecía que se la había robado de una chatarrería. Llevaba una camiseta cuyas mangas habían sido cortadas y unos pantalones de mezclilla bien gastados que habían sido cortados justo debajo de las rodillas. No llevaba calcetines dentro de sus sucios tenis de básquetbol.

Gran parte del peso de David se balanceaba en una pierna mientras estaba estacionando en la callejón entre la panadería y la florería. Todavía nos faltaba una cuadra para llegar a casa.

-Ponte detrás de mí, Joe, -dijo Mike y me jaló detrás de él. Yo tenía ocho años y jamás me movía tan rápido como mis hermanos querían.

Mi hermano mayor Gabe se paró al lado de Mike. Nuestra hermana Tina se acercó. Formaron una pared entre David y yo.

6

What Do Pronouns Do?

¿Cuál es la función de los pronombres?

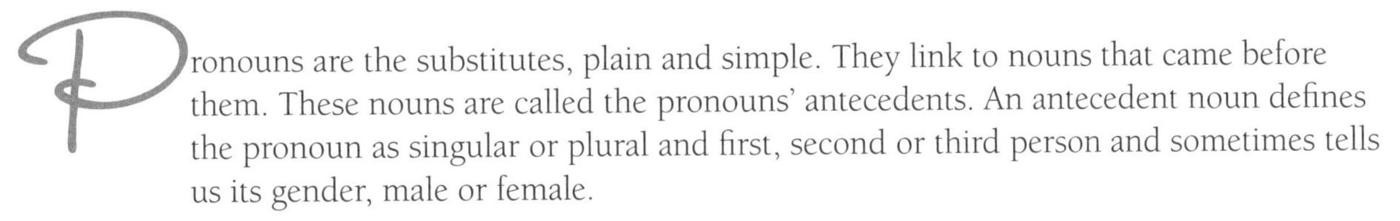

Pronouns are the substitutes, plain and simple. They link to nouns that came before them. These nouns are called the pronouns' antecedents. An antecedent noun defines the pronoun as singular or plural and first, second or third person and sometimes tells us its gender, male or female.

For example, when you write a story about Marsha, pronouns give you a way to say something other than *Marsha, Marsha, Marsha!* We don't have to repeat Marsha's name in an endless loop. Instead, we can call in a sub. Since Marsha is female, the substitute is *she* for Marsha. In fact, pronouns' main function is to give writers a way to clearly and consistently refer to characters or people without using their names over and over and over. The following lessons explore personal, second person, possessive, reflexive and indefinite pronouns.

Lesson Sets:

6.1 Los pronombres personales

6.2 Los pronombres en segunda persona

6.3 Los pronombres posesivos

6.4 Los pronombres reflexivos con verbos

6.5 Los pronombres indefinidos

Correlating English lessons for this chapter can be found in *Patterns of Power*, Chapter 10.

6.1 Los pronombres personales

Estándar Usar los pronombres personales y entender a quién se refieren.

Frase de enfoque Uso los pronombres personales.

Invitación a notar Sofía era tu abuela —él empezó—. Ella adoraba los libros, la poesía, las flores de jazmín, y, desde luego, me adoraba a mí. Fue ella quien me enseñó a leer.
—Juana Martínez-Neal, *Alma y cómo obtuvo su nombre*

Power Note *There are many skills that you might review with this sentence: dialogue, commas in a series, accents, past-tense you'll verbs, etc. Call students' attention to various pronouns (*él, ella, me, *y* mí*). You will find subjective (*tónicos*) pronouns and objective (*átonos*) pronouns in this sentence. But as Jeff says, we're preparing writers, not tiny linguists. It is unnecessary to differentiate between the types of pronouns for this lesson. It is, however, important to identify the person to which the pronouns refer.*

Invitación a comparar Sofía era tu abuela —él empezó—. Ella adoraba los libros, la poesía, las flores de jazmín, y, desde luego, me adoraba a mí. Fue ella quien me enseñó a leer.

Elizabeth era mi abuela. Ella adoraba la música, su familia y su hijo único, quien le enseñó a cantar.

Power Note *Ask students to point out the pronouns and identify to whom they refer. Students may note the possessive pronoun in both the original sentence and the imitation sentence. Acknowledge their noticings and use that when you teach Lesson 6.3.*

Invitación a imitar *Imitate Together:* Invite writers to use interactive or shared writing to compose a sentence with you. Offer students the story of your own name or speak about a certain member of your family.

> Celia es su abuela. A ella le gusta tejer, hacer crucigramas y platicar por teléfono con su nieto, quien la escucha atentamente.

Imitate Independently: Student pairs use the models to compose their own sentence, using pronouns with clear antecedents possibly about their own names or someone in their family.

Figure 6.1
A first grader experiments with pronouns in this paragraph about Cesar Chávez in the writers notebook

4-8
Cesar chabos form
Ellos tenian que vender
su rancho porque no tenian
nucho dinero y trabajaba en un
rancho y nomas les pagaban
treita sentabs

Invitación a celebrar

Students illustrate their sentences to show the person they wrote about. They can share these illustrated sentences with their classmates or their family.

Invitación a aplicar

In a subject other than language arts, students should look for sentences with pronouns in them. Practice linking pronouns back to the nouns to which they refer.

Invitación a corregir

¿Qué aprendimos de Juana Martínez-Neal acerca de la escritura?	
Sofía era tu abuela —él empezó—. Ella adoraba los libros, la poesía, las flores de jazmín, y, desde luego, me adoraba a mí. Fue ella quien me enseñó a leer.	
¿Qué ha cambiado? ¿Cuál es el efecto del cambio?	
(A) Sofía era tu abuela —Papá empezó—. Sofía adoraba los libros, la poesía, las flores de jazmín, y, desde luego, me adoraba a mí. Fue Sofía quien me enseñó a leer.	*Cuando reemplazamos los pronombres con el nombre* Sofía *las oraciones suenan repetitivas. No es necesario usar su nombre tantas veces si el lector ya sabe que estamos hablando de ella.*
(B) Ella era tu abuela —él empezó—. Ella adoraba los libros, la poesía, las flores de jazmín, y, desde luego, me adoraba a mí. Fue ella quien me enseñó a leer.	*Si usamos los pronombres sin haber dicho el nombre de la persona, el lector se queda con la duda de quién estamos hablando. A veces, es necesario decir el nombre de la persona para que las ideas queden claras.*
(C) Sofía era tu abuela él empezó. Ella adoraba los libros, la poesía, las flores de jazmín, y, desde luego, me adoraba a mí. Fue ella quien me enseñó a leer.	*Sin la raya, el lector no sabe que el papá está contando la historia de su mamá. Usamos las rayas para indicar diálogo.*

¿Qué notas?

Sofía era tu abuela —él empezó—. Ella adoraba los libros, la poesía, las flores de jazmín, y, desde luego, me adoraba a mí. Fue ella quien me enseñó a leer.

—Juana Martínez-Neal, *Alma y cómo obtuvo su nombre*

¿En qué se parecen? ¿En qué se diferencian?

Sofía era tu abuela —él empezó—. Ella adoraba los libros, la poesía, las flores de jazmín, y, desde luego, me adoraba a mí.
Fue ella quien me enseñó a leer.

Elizabeth era mi abuela. Ella adoraba la música, su familia y su hijo único, quien le enseñó a cantar.

Inténtalo

Sofía era tu abuela —él empezó—. Ella adoraba los libros, la poesía, las flores de jazmín, y, desde luego, me adoraba a mí. Fue ella quien me enseñó a leer.

Elizabeth era mi abuela. Ella adoraba la música, su familia y su hijo único, quien le ensenó a cantar.

Sofía era tu abuela —él empezó—. Ella adoraba los libros, la poesía, las flores de jazmín, y, desde luego, me adoraba a mí. Fue ella quien me enseñó a leer.

¿Qué ha cambiado? ¿Cuál es el efecto del cambio?

(A) Sofía era tu abuela —Papá empezó—. Sofía adoraba los libros, la poesía, las flores de jazmín, y, desde luego, me adoraba a mí. Fue Sofía quien me enseñó a leer.

(B) Ella era tu abuela —él empezó—. Ella adoraba los libros, la poesía, las flores de jazmín, y, desde luego, me adoraba a mí. Fue ella quien me enseñó a leer.

(C) Sofía era tu abuela él empezó. Ella adoraba los libros, la poesía, las flores de jazmín, y, desde luego, me adoraba a mí. Fue ella quien me enseñó a leer.

6.2 Los pronombres en segunda persona

Estándar Distinguir entre *tú y usted.*

Frase de enfoque Uso *usted* para indicar respeto.

Invitación a notar

—Buenos días, Lupe. ¿Cómo está usted? —dijo la señorita Jones muy despacio, pronunciando cada sílaba.

Sorprendida de que la maestra le hablara de un modo tan formal, Lupe no sabía cómo contestar. Pero sí sabía que debía mostrarse respetuosa y bajó la vista.

—Alma Flor Ada y Gabriel Zubizarreta, *Nacer bailando*

Power Note *Students may notice many things about this excerpt (dialogue, capitalization, question marks, etc.). Affirm all their noticings, but draw their attention to the word* usted. *Ask students, "¿Qué significa* usted?" *If students say it means* tú, *talk about why an author or a speaker might use* usted *instead of* tú.

Invitación a comparar

—Buenos días, Lupe. ¿Cómo está usted? —dijo la señorita Jones muy despacio, pronunciando cada sílaba.

Sorprendida de que la maestra le hablara de un modo tan formal, Lupe no sabía cómo contestar. Pero sí sabía que debía mostrarse respetuosa y bajó la vista.

—Hola, Lupe, ¿cómo estás? —dijo Camille en español, para practicar las frases que había estado usando en la Florida.

Power Note *This is another excerpt from the same book by Ada and Zubizarreta. Camille's dialogue uses an informal tone. Ask students why the same author would have two different characters speak to Lupe, the same character, with different tones.*

Invitación a imitar

Imitate Together: Invite writers to use interactive or shared writing to compose a message to the principal with you.

> Gracias, Sra. Santibañez, por apoyarnos en nuestra clase de escritura. Usted está invitada a nuestra celebración de autores el miércoles.

Imitate Independently: Students use the models to compose a sentence using *usted.* They can thinking about writing a message to someone in the school or community.

Invitación a celebrar Students read aloud their messages to the class. The class will confirm if they believe using a formal tone is appropriate for the message.

Invitación a aplicar Students should look for an opportunity during the school day in which they should interact with an adult in the school using *usted*. Discuss when and where these moments happen.

Invitación a corregir

¿Qué aprendimos de Alma Flor Ada y Gabriel Zubizarreta acerca de la escritura?	
—Buenos días, Lupe. ¿Cómo está usted? —dijo la señorita Jones muy despacio, pronunciando cada sílaba.	
¿Qué ha cambiado? ¿Cuál es el efecto del cambio?	
(A) —Buenos días, Lupe. ¿Cómo estás usted? —dijo la señorita Jones muy despacio, pronunciando cada sílaba.	*La conjugación estás es incorrecta porque, cuando usamos usted, empleamos la conjugación del verbo en tercera persona (está). Eso mantiene un tono formal.*
(B) Buenos días, Lupe. ¿Cómo está usted? dijo la señorita Jones muy despacio, pronunciando cada sílaba.	*Faltan las rayas que indican diálogo. Es confuso para el lector porque no va a saber exactamente qué palabras se dijeron.*
(C) —Buenos días, Lupe. Cómo está usted. —dijo la señorita Jones muy despacio, pronunciando cada sílaba.	*Faltan los signos de interrogación. Son necesarios porque requiere una respuesta.*

¿Qué notas?

—Buenos días, Lupe. ¿Cómo está usted? —dijo la señorita Jones muy despacio, pronunciando cada sílaba.

Sorprendida de que la maestra le hablara de un modo tan formal, Lupe no sabía cómo contestar. Pero sí sabía que debía mostrarse respetuosa y bajó la vista.

—Alma Flor Ada y Gabriel Zubizarreta, *Nacer bailando*

¿En qué se parecen? ¿En qué se diferencian?

—Buenos días, Lupe. ¿Cómo está usted? —dijo la señorita Jones muy despacio, pronunciando cada sílaba.

Sorprendida de que la maestra le hablara de un modo tan formal, Lupe no sabía cómo contestar. Pero sí sabía que debía mostrarse respetuosa y bajó la vista.

—Hola, Lupe, ¿cómo estás? —dijo Camille en español, para practicar las frases que había estado usando en la Florida.

Inténtalo

—Buenos días, Lupe. ¿Cómo está usted? —dijo la señorita Jones muy despacio, pronunciando cada sílaba.

Sorprendida de que la maestra le hablara de un modo tan formal, Lupe no sabía cómo contestar. Pero sí sabía que debía mostrarse respetuosa y bajó la vista.

—Hola, Lupe, ¿cómo estás? —dijo Camille en español, para practicar las frases que había estado usando en la Florida.

—Buenos días, Lupe. ¿Cómo está usted? —dijo la señorita Jones muy despacio, pronunciando cada sílaba.

¿Qué ha cambiado? ¿Cuál es el efecto del cambio?

(A) —Buenos días, Lupe. ¿Cómo estás usted? —dijo la señorita Jones muy despacio, pronunciando cada sílaba.

(B) Buenos días, Lupe. ¿Cómo está usted? dijo la señorita Jones muy despacio, pronunciando cada sílaba.

(C) —Buenos días, Lupe. Cómo está usted. —dijo la señorita Jones muy despacio, pronunciando cada sílaba.

6.3 Los pronombres posesivos

Estándar Usar y entender los pronombres posesivos.

Frase de enfoque Uso los pronombres posesivos.

Invitación a notar A mi mamá y a mí nos gusta escribirle cartas a nuestra familia y a nuestros amigos.
—Jorge Ramos, *Me parezco tanto a mi mamá*

Power Note *If students are not noticing the possessive pronouns, encourage them to analyze what comes right before some of the nouns in the sentence. To reinforce the idea that possessive pronouns agree with their nouns in gender and number, compare* nuestros *y* nuestra *and the nouns that follow.*

Invitación a comparar A mi mamá y a mí nos gusta escribirle cartas a nuestra familia y a nuestros amigos.

A mis abuelos les gusta ver películas de sus tiempos.

Power Note *As students point out the possessive pronouns in this imitation, ask students why the author uses* mi *but the imitation uses* mis. *Students should note that the noun decides how we use our possessive pronouns.*

Invitación a imitar *Imitate Together:* Invite writers to use interactive or shared writing to compose a sentence with you.

¿Me prestas tu libro?

Imitate in Pairs: Student pairs use the models to compose their own sentence, using pronouns with clear antecedents about any subject they choose.

Invitación a celebrar Students share their sentences aloud, reading them twice. Applaud writers for the hard work of making their prounouns agree with their nouns.

Invitación a aplicar Students write about getting dressed using possessive pronouns (*mis zapatos, mi camisa*, etc.).

Invitación a corregir

¿Qué aprendimos de Jorge Ramos acerca de la escritura?	
A mi mamá y a mí nos gusta escribirle cartas a nuestra familia y a nuestros amigos.	
¿Qué ha cambiado? ¿Cuál es el efecto del cambio?	
(A) A tu mamá y a ti les gusta escribirle cartas a nuestra familia y a nuestros amigos.	*Los pronombres han cambiado a segunda persona* (tu). *Ahora no concuerdan con* nuestra *y* nuestros, *que describen a la familia y las cartas.*
(B) A mi mamá y a mí nos gusta escribirle cartas a su familia y a sus amigos.	*Los pronombres posesivos han cambiado a* su *y* sus, *lo cual indica que la familia y los amigos pertenecen a otros.*
(C) A mi mamá y a mí nos gustó escribirle cartas a nuestra familia y a nuestros amigos.	*La conjugación de* gustar *cambió, lo cual indica que fue una actividad que les gustó en el pasado pero no hoy en día.*

¿Qué notas?

A mi mamá y a mí nos gusta escribirle cartas a nuestra familia y a nuestros amigos.

—Jorge Ramos, *Me parezco tanto a mi mamá*

¿En qué se parecen? ¿En qué se diferencian?

A mi mamá y a mí nos gusta escribirle cartas a nuestra familia y a nuestros amigos.

A mis abuelos les gusta ver películas de sus tiempos.

Inténtalo

A mi mamá y a mí nos gusta escribirle cartas a nuestra familia y a nuestros amigos.

A mis abuelos les gusta ver películas de sus tiempos.

A mi mamá y a mí nos gusta escribirle cartas a nuestra familia y a nuestros amigos.

¿Qué ha cambiado? ¿Cuál es el efecto del cambio?

(A) A tu mamá y a ti les gusta escribirle cartas a nuestra familia y a nuestros amigos.

(B) A mi mamá y a mí nos gusta escribirle cartas a su familia y a sus amigos.

(C) A mi mamá y a mí nos gustó escribirle cartas a nuestra familia y a nuestros amigos.

6.4 Los pronombres reflexivos con verbos

Estándar Usar los pronombres reflexivos para completar los verbos reflexivos.

Frase de enfoque Uso los pronombres reflexivos con los verbos reflexivos.

Invitación a notar Popoca se negó a moverse. Se quedó junto a Izta, como se lo había prometido cuando la conoció.
—Duncan Tonatiuh, *La princesa y el guerrero*

Power Note *In Spanish, reflexive pronouns accompany reflexive verbs. In this model, we find three examples of reflexive verbs with reflexive pronouns (*negarse, moverse, *and* quedarse*).*

Invitación a comparar Popoca se negó a moverse. Se quedó junto a Izta, como se lo había prometido cuando la conoció.

Mi hermano se despertó para meterse a bañar. Él sentía que no podía quitarse el olor a zorrillo que se encontró ayer.

Power Note *Reflexive pronouns let us know that the action is performed for or by the subject on themselves. Generate a list of verbs that are commonly reflexive. Have students think about verbs that often go along with* se, me, te, *or* nos.

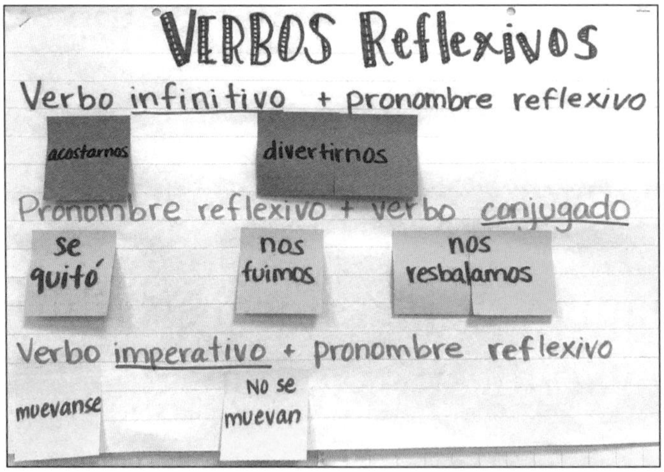

Figure 6.4a
Collecting reflexive verbs

Invitación a imitar

Invite students to use the chart you generated together to create sentences in pairs. Encourage various patterns of the use of reflexive pronouns. Here are some examples:

¡Péinate!
No se quería peinar.
No quería peinarse.
No se peinó.

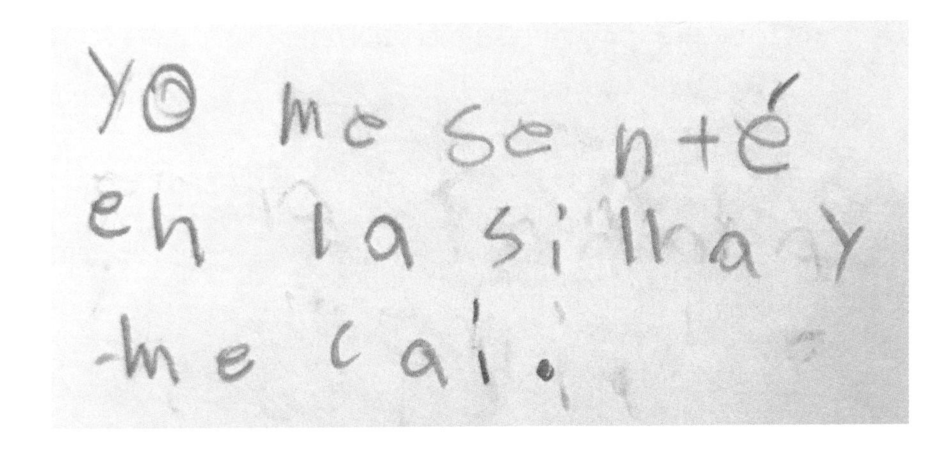

Figure 6.4b
A student experiments with reflexive pronouns

Invitación a celebrar

Have pairs share out their sentences. Note all the variations that students use with reflexive pronouns with reflexive verbs. Add any verbs to the chart that students use that you had not listed yet.

Invitación a aplicar

Scavenger Hunt. Have students collect sentences on notecards from their independent reading where they can find reflexive verbs. Add these sentences to your reflexive verbs chart.

Invitación a corregir

¿Qué aprendimos de Duncan Tontiuh acerca de la escritura?	
Popoca se negó a moverse. Se quedó junto a Izta, como se lo había prometido cuando la conoció.	
¿Qué ha cambiado? ¿Cuál es el efecto del cambio?	
(A) Popoca se negó a mover. Se quedó junto a Izta, como se lo había prometido cuando la conoció.	*Sin el* se, *mover ya no existe como un verbo reflexivo. Al usar* moverse, *estamos seguros, como lectores, de que el personaje de Popoca no se va mover físicamente de este lugar.*
(B) Popoca te negó a moverte. Te quedó junto a Izta, como se lo había prometido cuando la conoció.	Te *no es el pronombre reflexivo apropriado en este caso. Como el texto esta escrito en tercera persona, los pronombres reflexivos necesitan concordar con el sujeto de la oración.*
(C) Popoca negó a mover. Quedó junto a Izta, como se lo había prometido cuando la conoció.	*Los verbos* negarse, moverse *y* quedarse *suelen escribirse como verbos reflexivos. Las oraciones pierden su fluidez cuando se las lee.*

¿Qué notas?

Popoca se negó a moverse. Se quedó junto a Izta, como se lo había prometido cuando la conoció.

—Duncan Tonatiuh, *La princesa y el guerrero*

¿En qué se parecen? ¿En qué se diferencian?

Popoca se negó a moverse. Se quedó junto a Izta, como se lo había prometido cuando la conoció.

Mi hermano se despertó para meterse a bañar. Él sentía que no podía quitarse el olor a zorrillo que se encontró ayer.

Inténtalo

Popoca se negó a moverse. Se quedó junto a Izta, como se lo había prometido cuando la conoció.

Mi hermano se despertó para meterse a bañar. Él sentía que no podía quitarse el olor a zorrillo que se encontró ayer.

Popoca se negó a moverse. Se quedó junto a Izta, como se lo había prometido cuando la conoció.

¿Qué ha cambiado? ¿Cuál es el efecto del cambio?

(A) Popoca se negó a mover. Se quedó junto a Izta, como se lo había prometido cuando la conoció.

(B) Popoca te negó a moverte. Te quedó junto a Izta, como se lo había prometido cuando la conoció.

(C) Popoca negó a mover. Quedó junto a Izta, como se lo había prometido cuando la conoció.

6.5 Los pronombres indefinidos

Estándar Usar y entender los pronombres indefinidos.

Frase de enfoque Uso los pronombres indefinidos.

Invitación a notar

Los pronombres indefinidos de *El caso de la pluma perdida*	
Todos	Todos estaban en silencio. Era como si todos hubieran parado de respirar. Todos los ojos estaban sobre mí.
Algo	Si algo he aprendido en el par de años que llevo resolviendo crímenes es que si una persona repite una y otra vez que no hizo algo, lo más probable es que sí lo haya hecho.
Nadie	Detrás de Eddy estaba Bucho, dándole palmaditas en el hombro, diciéndole en voz baja que nadie se iría hoy hasta que apareciera la pluma.
Ninguno	Todos celebraron. Ninguno más fuerte que Toots.
Todas las oraciones están en *El caso de la pluma perdida* de René Saldaña, Jr.	

Power Note *Indefinite pronouns need no antecedent. In the case of Mickey Rangel, the main character in the book by René Saldaña, Jr., he is solving crime in school and, therefore, we make assumptions about who the indefinite pronouns refer to.*

Invitación a comparar Todos estaban en silencio. Era como si todos hubieran parado de respirar. Todos los ojos estaban sobre mí.

Nadie habló. Era como si todos estaban tan interesados en lo que iba a decir. Pero no podía decir nada.

Power Note *Emphasize that* nadie *and* nada *indicate the absense of a person or thing. Therefore, we won't find an antecedent in the text.*

Invitación a imitar *Imitate Together:* Invite writers compose a sentence with a partner using at least one indefinite pronoun. A chart of indefinite pronouns is helpful: *uno, alguien, algo, algún, alguno, algunos, nadie, nada, ningún, ninguno, ningunos, etc.*

Imitate Independently: Students use the models to compose their own sentence, using indefinite pronouns.

Invitación a celebrar Students share their sentences aloud, reading them twice. Applaud writers for working hard on using indefinite pronouns.

Invitación a aplicar Have students work in groups to write about changes they would like to see at school (a nadie le gusta tarea, todos quireron más recreo, etc.).

Invitación a corregir

¿Qué aprendimos de René Saldaña, Jr. acerca de la escritura?	
Todos estaban en silencio. Era como si todos hubieran parado de respirar. Todos los ojos estaban sobre mí.	
¿Qué ha cambiado? ¿Cuál es el efecto del cambio?	
(A) Todo estaban en silencio. Era como si todos hubieran parado de respirar. Todos los ojos estaban sobre mí.	Todo *está escrito sin la* s. *Ahora el pronombre indefinido y el verbo no concuerdan. Los pronombres y verbos tienen que concordar en cantidad.*
(B) Todos estaban en silencio. Era como si todos hubiera parado de respirar. Todos los ojos estaban sobre mí.	*El verbo* hubiera *está escrito en su forma singular. El pronombre indefinido* todos *es plural y tiene que concordar con el verbo.*
(C) Todos estaban en silencio. Era como si todos hubieran parado de respirar. Todo los ojos estaban sobre mí.	*Para describir* los ojos, *el autor usó* todos. *Como es una idea plural, los adjetivos tienen que concordar en cantidad.*

¿Qué patrones se notan con estos pronombres indefinidos?

Los pronombres indefinidos de *El caso de la pluma perdida*	
Todos	Todos estaban en silencio. Era como si todos hubieran parado de respirar. Todos los ojos estaban sobre mí.
Algo	Si algo he aprendido en el par de años que llevo resolviendo crímenes es que si una persona repite una y otra vez que no hizo algo, lo más probable es que sí lo haya hecho.
Nadie	Detrás de Eddy estaba Bucho, dándole palmaditas en el hombro, diciéndole en voz baja que nadie se iría hoy hasta que apareciera la pluma.
Ninguno	Todos celebraron. Ninguno más fuerte que Toots.
Todas las oraciones están en *El caso de la pluma perdida por* René Saldaña, Jr.	

¿En qué se parecen? ¿En qué se diferencian?

Todos estaban en silencio. Era como si todos hubieran parado de respirar. Todos los ojos estaban sobre mí.

Nadie habló. Era como si todos estaban tan interesados en lo que iba a decir. Pero no podía decir nada.

Inténtalo

Todos estaban en silencio. Era como si todos hubieran parado de respirar. Todos los ojos estaban sobre mí.

Nadie habló. Era como si todos estaban tan interesados en lo que iba a decir. Pero no podía decir nada.

Todos estaban en silencio. Era como si todos hubieran parado de respirar. Todos los ojos estaban sobre mí.

¿Qué ha cambiado? ¿Cuál es el efecto del cambio?

(A) Todo estaban en silencio. Era como si todos hubieran parado de respirar. Todos los ojos estaban sobre mí.

(B) Todos estaban en silencio. Era como si todos hubiera parado de respirar. Todos los ojos estaban sobre mí.

(C) Todos estaban en silencio. Era como si todos hubieran parado de respirar. Todo los ojos estaban sobre mí.

7

How Do Verbs and Nouns Agree?

¿Cómo se relacionan los verbos y los sustantivos?

In every sentence, nouns and verbs work side by side to create an unbroken sense of meaning. And to work well together, they have to stay in agreement. The subjects of our sentences directly dictate what form our verbs will take. Writers have to stay on their toes here and think about matching nouns—whether singular or plural—with their correlating verbs. Though pairing verbs with nouns correctly may come easier while speaking, young writers often need extra support monitoring for this when putting pen to paper. This can be especially true when working with implicit subjects in Spanish, so you'll find some extra support for *sujetos tácitos* in Lesson 7.3.

In the end, verbs standing in agreement make reading clear and easy to follow. When nouns and verbs are not in agreement, it can make our prose sputter or clang, and make our readers look for something less disagreeable to read.

Lesson Sets:

7.1 Los sustantivos y verbos como amigos

7.2 La concordancia entre sustantivos y verbos

7.3 Los sujetos tácitos

7.4 Buscar los verbos que concuerdan en cantidad y persona

Correlating English lessons for this chapter can be found in *Patterns of Power*, Chapter 11.

7.1 Los sustantivos y verbos como amigos

Estándar Usar verbos que concuerdan con los sustantivos singulares o plurales.

Frase de enfoque Me aseguro que los verbos y sustantivos son amigos.

Power Note *Read aloud Pat Mora's poem "Chocolate." You may read it multiple times and have students repeat the invitation-to-notice sentence with you several times: "Tus ojos bailan."*

Invitación a notar Tus ojos bailan.
—Pat Mora, "Chocolate" del libro *Yum! ¡Mmm! ¡Qué Rico!*

Power Note ¿Esta oración ocurre en el presente? ¿U ocurrió en el pasado? ¿Cómo sabes? *Students might be able to express that the sentence is written in present tense by telling you what it might sound like in past tense (*Tus ojos bailaron*).*

Invitación a comparar Tus ojos bailan.

Tu nariz lo huele.

Power Note *These sentences provide a good opportunity to not only review how nouns and verbs work together, but also how adjectives must agree with nouns.*

Invitación a imitar *Imitate Together:* Invite writers to use interactive or shared writing to compose a sentence with you.

Imitate in Pairs: Students use the model sentences to compose a sentence in which the nouns and verbs agree. Say, "Asegúrense que pueden explicar por qué o cómo los verbos y sustantivos concuerdan en sus oraciones."

Figures 7.1a and b
Fourth graders write simple sentences

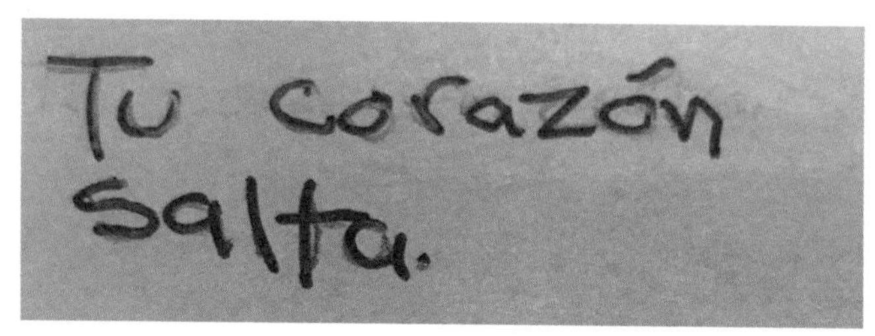

Tus pies se
mueven.

Invitación a celebrar

Students share their sentences aloud or on a document camera, explaining how they know that the nouns and verbs agree.

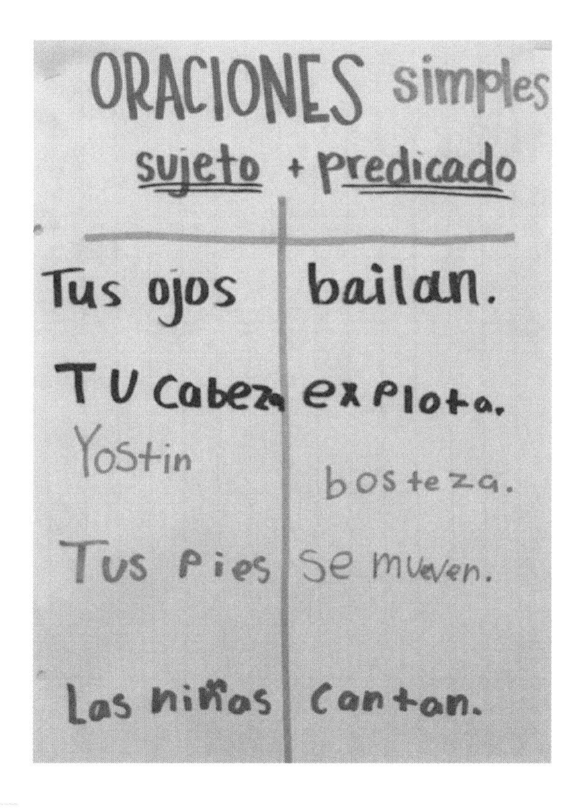

Figure 7.1c
Class chart with simple sentences showing subject-verb agreement

Invitación a aplicar

Writers return to a recent piece of writing and check for subject-verb agreement with a partner. After they help each other, debrief by asking, "¿Qué notaron? ¿En qué necesitamos enfocarnos como escritores?"

Invitación a corregir

¿Qué aprendimos de Pat Mora acerca de la escritura?	
Tus ojos bailan.	
¿Qué ha cambiado? ¿Cuál es el efecto del cambio?	
(A) Tus ojos baila.	*El verbo* baila *no concuerda con el sustantivo* ojos. *Un sustantivo plural requiere un verbo como* bailan.
(B) Tu ojos bailan.	*La palabra* tu *debe describir* ojos. *Como* ojos *es un sustantivo plural, requiere la palabra* tus.
(C) Tus ojos bailando.	*La palabra* bailando *necesita otro verbo. Sin la palabra* están, *no suena bien.*

¿Qué notas?

Tus ojos bailan.

—Pat Mora, "Chocolate" del libro *Yum! ¡Mmm! ¡Qué Rico!*

¿En qué se parecen? ¿En qué se diferencian?

Tus ojos bailan.

Tu nariz lo huele.

Inténtalo

Tus ojos bailan.

Tu nariz lo huele.

Tus ojos bailan.

¿Qué ha cambiado? ¿Cuál es el efecto del cambio?

(A) Tus ojos baila.

(B) Tu ojos bailan.

(C) Tus ojos bailando.

7.2 La concordancia entre sustantivos y verbos

Estándar Crear concordancia entre los sustantivos y los verbos en las oraciones

Frase de enfoque Me aseguro que los verbos concuerdan con los sustantivos.

Invitación a notar Creo que después de que murió tu abuela, muchas de las viejas tradiciones también murieron.
—Raina Telgemeier, *Fantasmas*

Power Note *If students are still noting the basics of a sentence (capital letter at the beginning, period at the end, etc.) spend less time emphasizing and restating students' noticings. Simply say, "Sí. ¿Qué más?" If students are not using the words singular and plural (cognates in Spanish), review with students the meanings so they are able to speak about the subject-verb agreement. In this sentence the conjugation of* morir *changes based on the noun near it.*

Invitación a comparar Creo que después de que murió tu abuela, muchas de las viejas tradiciones también murieron.

Nuestra abuela nos enseñó a hacer tamales y ahora te enseñamos a ti.

Power Note *In the imitation, we also repeat the same verb in order to call attention to how the verb changes according to its subject. Encourage students to name why the verb changes.*

Invitación a imitar *Imitate Together:* Invite writers to use interactive or shared writing to compose a sentence with you.

> En la clase escribimos poemas a nuestros amigos, así que yo te escribí uno.

Imitate in Pairs: Students use the model sentences to compose a sentence in which the nouns and verbs agree. Say, "Asegúrense que pueden explicar por qué o cómo los verbos y sustantivos concuerdan en sus oraciones."

Invitación a celebrar Student pairs share their sentences with the class. The authors of the sentence ask their classmates to explain why their nouns and verbs match. The authors should agree or disagree and explain.

Invitación a aplicar Writers look at their own writing to check for subject-verb agreement with a partner. After helping each other, ask "¿Qué notaron? ¿Tienen dudas? ¿A qué debemos prestar atención como autores y lectores?"

Invitación a corregir

¿Qué aprendimos de Raina Telgemeier acerca de la escritura?	
Creo que después de que murió tu abuela, muchas de las viejas tradiciones también murieron.	
¿Qué ha cambiado? Cuál es el efecto del cambio?	
(A) Creo que después de que murieron tu abuela, muchas de las viejas tradiciones también murieron.	*La primera conjugación del verbo* morir *se refiere a un sustantivo plural. Sin embargo, el sustantivo* abuela *es singular.*
(B) Creo que después de que murió tu abuela, muchas de las viejas tradiciones también murió.	*La segunda conjugación del verbo* morir *se refiere a un sustantivo singular. Sin embargo, el sustantivo* tradiciones *es plural.*
(C) Creo que después de que murió tus abuelos, muchas de las viejas tradiciones también murieron.	*Se cambió* abuela *por* abuelos. *Ahora, el sustantivo plural requiere otra conjugación del verbo* morir.

¿Qué notas?

Creo que después de que murió tu abuela, muchas de las viejas tradiciones también murieron.

—Raina Telgemeier, *Fantasmas*

¿En qué se parecen? ¿En qué se diferencian?

Creo que después de que murió tu abuela, muchas de las viejas tradiciones también murieron.

Nuestra abuela nos enseñó a hacer tamales y ahora te enseñamos a ti.

Inténtalo

Creo que después de que murió tu abuela, muchas de las viejas tradiciones también murieron.

Nuestra abuela nos enseñó a hacer tamales y ahora te enseñamos a ti.

En el invierno, está bajo y tranquilo. En el verano, está lleno y ruidoso.

¿Qué ha cambiado? ¿Cuál es el efecto del cambio?

(A) Creo que después de que murieron tu abuela, muchas de las viejas tradiciones también murieron.

(B) Creo que después de que murió tu abuela, muchas de las viejas tradiciones también murió.

(C) Creo que después de que murió tus abuelos, muchas de las viejas tradiciones también murieron.

7.3 Los sujetos tácitos

Estándar Identificar y usar las oraciones simples con un sujeto tácito.

Frase de enfoque Escribo oraciones simples con el sujeto tácito para no ser repetitivo.

Invitación a notar Tenían las manos pegajosas de masa.
—Gary Soto, *¡Qué montón de tamales!*

Power Note *If you have taught that the simple sentence must have a subject and a predicate, the idea of* sujetos tácitos *in Spanish can be difficult. Ask students if they believe that this is a complete sentence. To illustrate that this sentence can stand alone, try replacing* tenían *with* tener. *Students will likely hear that the infinitive verb causes this sentence to be incomplete, while the conjugated verb* tenían *indicates that there is indeed an implicit subject in the verb conjugation.*

Invitación a comparar Tenían las manos pegajosas de masa.

María y su mamá tenían las manos pegajosas de masa.

Ellas tenían las manos pegajosas de masa.

Power Note *In this invitation to compare, we choose to rewrite the sentence stating the subject explicitly and then stating the subject using a pronoun. We want to emphasize that all of these examples constitute a complete simple sentence. As readers, we have to look at previous sentences to understand the subject of simple sentences without explicit subjects. As writers, we must make sure our readers can deduce who the explicit subject is without restating it.*

Here is the original excerpt from Gary Soto's ¡Qué montón de tamales!:

> María despegó la nariz del cristal de la ventana y regresó al mostrador de la cocina. Se estaba portando como una niña grande, ayudando a su madre a hacer tamales. Tenían las manos pegajosas de masa.

Invitación a imitar *Imitate Together:* Invite students to use interactive or shared writing to compose a sentence with you.

> Ayudé a mi abuela a hacer chocolate caliente. Tomamos nuestra bebida en tazas de café.

Imitate Independently: Students should write two or more sentences in which they use at least one *sujeto tácito*. Students should check with a peer that the reader can still understand who the subject of the sentence is, even when it's not stated.

Figure 7.3a
Anchor chart with three examples that express the same idea in different ways.

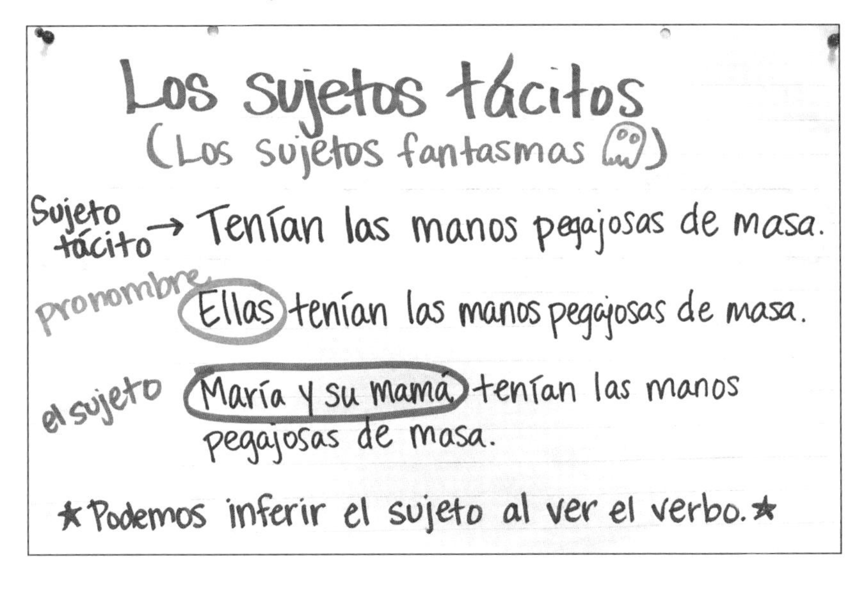

Figure 7.3b
A first grader writes using *un sujeto tácito* in the sentence, "No quiere su vacuna."

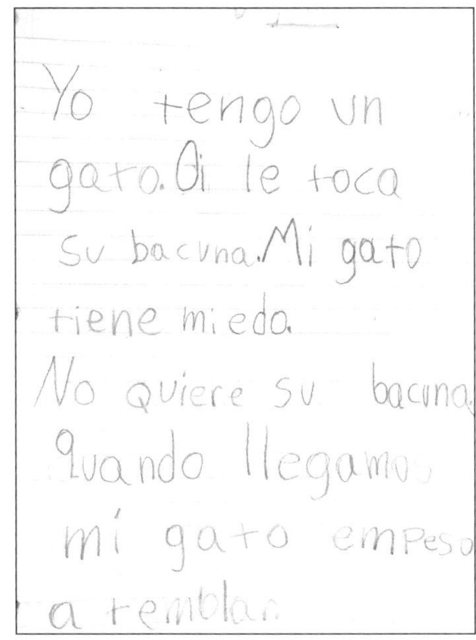

Invitación a celebrar Have students read their sentences aloud. Students should tell the student author what they believe the subject is. The author will confirm if they are correct.

Invitación a aplicar *Scavenger Hunt.* Have students collect simple sentences with implicit subjects from their independent reading and jot them on note cards. Display these on a *Sujetos tácitos* Chart.

Invitación a corregir

¿Qué aprendimos de Gary Soto acerca de la escritura?	
Tenían las manos pegajosas de masa.	
¿Qué ha cambiado? ¿Cuál es el efecto del cambio?	
(A) Tenían las manos pegajosos de masa.	*El adjetivo* pegajosos *se refiere a un sustantivo masculino. La palabra* manos *es irregular en que es un sustantivo femenino. Los adjetivos tienen que concordar con los sustantivos que describen.*
(C) Tenía las manos pegajosas de masa.	*El verbo* tenía *se refiere a un sujeto singular. Como vimos, las oraciones previas indican que son dos personas que están amasando.*
(B) Tener las manos pegajosas de masa.	*Al usar el verbo infinitivo, se pierde el sujeto tácito. Cuando el verbo no está conjugado, no sabemos quién está haciendo la acción.*

¿Qué notas?

Tenían las manos pegajosas de masa.
—Gary Soto, ¡Qué montón de tamales!

¿En qué se parecen? ¿En qué se diferencian?

Tenían las manos pegajosas de masa.

María y su mamá tenían las manos pegajosas de masa.

Ellas tenían las manos pegajosas de masa.

Inténtalo

Tenían las manos pegajosas de masa.

María y su mamá tenian las manos pegajosas de masa.

Ellas tenían las manos pegajosas de masa.

Tenían las manos pegajosas de masa.

¿Qué ha cambiado? ¿Cuál es el efecto del cambio?

(A) Tenían las manos pegajosos de masa.

(B) Tenía las manos pegajosas de masa.

(C) Tener las manos pegajosas de masa.

7.4 Buscar los verbos que concuerdan en cantidad y persona

Estándar Reconocer y corregir cuando los verbos no concuerdan con los sustantivos en las oraciones.

Frase de enfoque Mis verbos concuerdan con mis sustantivos.

Invitación a notar

Power Note *We change our lesson format for this one. We want students to be able to sustain a verb tense throughout a piece of writing. We use a cloze activity where we have omitted the verbs.*

First give students this handout (Ficha A-7.4) with an excerpt from Los tamales de Ana *by Gwendolyn Zepeda and have them fill in the verbs using the cards you have cut out from Ficha B-7.4. Ask, "¿En qué tenemos que pensar mientras trabajamos en esto?"* and use this text: (Debe tener sentido y los verbos y sustantivos tienen que concordar. Nos tenemos que fijar en los tiempos verbales. Normalmente, usamos un solo tiempo verbal.)

Invitación a comparar Show students the original text the cloze activity was taken from (Ficha C-7.4) and think about why the author made the choices she did.

Invitación a imitar Students brainstorm the things they will be able to do when they are a year or two older. They should use the space on Ficha C-7.4 to imitate Zepeda's paragraphs.

Invitación a celebrar Students read their paragraphs to their table partners, listening to each other for noun and verb agreement and consistency of tense.

Ficha A: Lección 7.4

Instrucciones: Con su grupo, lean los dos parráfos y agreguen el verbo que tenga sentido en cada espacio en blanco. ¿En qué necesitan pensar?

Cuando ______ los ocho, ______ bastante grande como para hacer muchas cosas nuevas. ______ palabras largas. ______ lugares altos. ______ en mi bicicleta sin las rueditas de entrenamiento.

Cuando ______ los catorce, la gente me ______ confianza para todo. Mis primos me ______ cargar a sus bebés sin tener que sentarme en el sillón. Papi me ______ regar sus plantas yo solita. Cuando vayamos a la gasolinera, Mami me ______ presionar los botones para pagar con la tarjeta de crédito y me ______ poner gasolina.

Ficha B: Lección 7.4

Instrucciones para el maestro: Antes de enseñar esta lección, copia un juego de palabras por cada grupo. Corta las palabras sin dejar mucho espacio en blanco. Pon cada juego dentro de un sobre.

cumpla	cumpliré	cumplí
soy	seré	era
leo	leeré	leí
alcanzo	alcanzaré	alcancé
ando	andaré	andaba
cumpla	cumpliré	cumplí
tiene	tendrá	tenía
dejan	dejarán	dejaron
deja	dejará	dejó
deja	dejará	dejó
deja	dejará	dejó

Distribuye los sobres a cada grupo con las palabras cortadas. Los estudiantes deben seguir estos pasos:

- Pongan todas las palabras de frente en la mesa.
- Agrupen las palabras en tres categorias (por lo menos).
- Platiquen acerca de cómo decidieron a agruparlas.
- Escojan qué verbos deben estar en los espacios en blanco.
- Platiquen acerca de por qué decidieron usar los verbos que escogieron.

Ficha C: Lección 7.4

Cuando cumpla los ocho, seré bastante grande como para hacer muchas cosas nuevas. Leeré palabras largas. Alcanzaré lugares altos. Andaré en mi bicicleta sin las rueditas de entrenamiento.

Cuando cumpla los catorce, la gente me tendrá confianza para todo. Mis primos me dejarán cargar a sus bebés sin tener que sentarme en el sillón. Papi me dejará regar sus plantas yo solita. Cuando vayamos a la gasolinera, Mami me dejará presionar los botones para pagar con la tarjeta de crédito y me dejará poner gasolina.

8

How Do Writers Use Dialogue and Parentheses?

¿Cómo los escritores usan el diálogo y los paréntesis?

The lessons included in this set introduce writers to two ways they can add clarity and detail to their writing through dialogue and parenthesis.

In Spanish, writers us a long dash, or *la raya,* to signal that two or more people are engaged in a conversation. As your students begin to notice language patterns for the ways Spanish indicates dialogue it may spark some lively discussions about how these differ from their English counterpart. Allow for this. Comparing and noticing differences between their two languages is a fun and vital part of being bilingual learners.

And who could pass up a sweet pair of parentheses? Parentheses are like potato chips. You can't just have one. Writers quickly understand that, if you open with one, you'll need to close with the other. Pairs of parentheses aren't used as often in fiction as in nonfiction but they always give the author a way to efficiently add clarifying information (definitions, examples, asides).

Lesson Sets:

8.1 El diálogo

8.2 Los paréntesis

Correlating English lessons for this chapter can be found in *Patterns of Power*, Chapter 12.

8.1 El diálogo

Estándar Usar la raya para indicar diálogo.

Frase de enfoque Uso la raya cuando dos o más personas están hablando.

Invitación a notar —¿Vendrá abuelita a mi fiesta? —le pregunto a mami. Esta vez, ella no sonríe.

—Marisol, no es solo el dinero —explica mami—. Es difícil conseguir los papeles necesarios para venir a Estados Unidos. Abuelita necesita un documento especial llamado *visa* para visitarnos y, a veces, las visas demoran mucho en llegar.

—Monica Brown, *Marisol McDonald y la fiesta sin igual*

Power Note *Even though students may notice several conventions of dialogue, focus mostly on the use of* la raya. *In this Invitation to Notice, we see an example of spoken words followed by the attribution* (le pregunto a mami) *where the spoken words end. In the second part, we see an example of how spoken words continue after the attribution. It might help students to highlight the spoken words to separate the dialogue from the narration.*

Invitación a comparar —¿Vendrá abuelita a mi fiesta? —le pregunto a mami. Esta vez, ella no sonríe.

—Marisol, no es solo el dinero —explica mami—. Es difícil conseguir los papeles necesarios para venir a Estados Unidos. Abuelita necesita un documento especial llamado *visa* para visitarnos y, a veces, las visas demoran mucho en llegar.

Entro al estudio y allí, en la pantalla de la computadora, ¡está abuelita!

—Feliz cumpleaños, Marisol —dice ella, y ambas nos reímos—. Sigo esperando por mi visa, pero utilicé parte del dinero que me enviaste para comprar mi primera computadora y obtener una conexión de internet. Ahora podremos hablar y cantar juntas, y podré ver tu cara bonita todo el tiempo.

Power Note *This Invitation to Compare and Contrast comes from the same book by Monica Brown. Have students compare and contrast the sentences that use dialogue and those that don't. Also discuss how dialogue is punctuated. List students' noticings about dialogue, creating a list of dialogue patterns. It might be difficult for students to understand that narration from a first-person point-of-view is not considered dialogue.*

Invitación a imitar

Imitate Together: Invite students to compose a few sentences of dialogue, focusing on the placement of *la raya.* Writers may use a class generated list of conventions to refine their dialogue.

Imitate in Pairs: Students work in pairs using the model to create their own sentence.

Invitación a celebrar

Pairs rehearse and perform their sentences with dialogue.

Invitación a aplicar

Writers should look at a narrative piece from their writing folder or notebook and ask themselves, "Did I use dialogue?" "What do I know now that I didn't know then?" "Do I need to make any changes?"

Invitación a corregir

¿Qué aprendimos de Monica Brown acerca de la escritura?	
—¿Vendrá abuelita a mi fiesta? —le pregunto a mami. Esta vez, ella no sonríe.	
¿Qué ha cambiado? ¿Cuál es el efecto del cambio?	
(A) ¿Vendrá abuelita a mi fiesta? le pregunto a mami. Esta vez, ella no sonríe.	*Las rayas no están escritas para indicar que alguien está hablando. Esto es confuso para los lectores porque es difícil distinguir entre oraciones normales y las del diálogo.*
(B) —¿Vendrá abuelita a mi fiesta? le pregunto a mami. Esta vez, ella no sonríe.	*La raya empieza las palabras habladas, pero no las cierra. El lector no sabe dónde terminan las palabras que alguien dijo.*
(C) —Vendrá abuelita a mi fiesta —le pregunto a mami. Esta vez, ella no sonríe.	*Faltan los signos de interrogación. Sin los signos de interrogación, suena como una oración declarativa.*

¿Qué notas?

—¿Vendrá abuelita a mi fiesta? —le pregunto a mami. Esta vez, ella no sonríe.

—Marisol, no es solo el dinero —explica mami—. Es difícil conseguir los papeles necesarios para venir a Estados Unidos.

Abuelita necesita un documento especial llamado *visa* para visitarnos y, a veces, las visas demoran mucho en llegar.
—Monica Brown, *Marisol McDonald y la fiesta sin igual*

¿En qué se parecen? ¿En qué se diferencian?

—¿Vendrá abuelita a mi fiesta? —le pregunto a mami. Esta vez, ella no sonríe.

—Marisol, no es solo el dinero —explica mami—. Es difícil conseguir los papeles necesarios para venir a Estados Unidos. Abuelita necesita un documento especial llamado *visa* para visitarnos y, a veces, las visas demoran mucho en llegar.

Entro al estudio y allí, en la pantalla de la computadora, ¡está abuelita!

—Feliz cumpleaños, Marisol —dice ella, y ambas nos reímos—. Sigo esperando por mi visa, pero utilicé parte del dinero que me enviaste para comprar mi primera computadora y obtener una conexión de internet. Ahora podremos hablar y cantar juntas, y podré ver tu cara bonita todo el tiempo.

Inténtalo

—¿Vendrá abuelita a mi fiesta? —le pregunto a mami. Esta vez, ella no sonríe.

—Marisol, no es solo el dinero —explica mami—. Es difícil conseguir los papeles necesarios para venir a Estados Unidos. Abuelita necesita un documento especial llamado *visa* para visitarnos y, a veces, las visas demoran mucho en llegar.

Entro al estudio y allí, en la pantalla de la computadora, ¡está abuelita!

—Feliz cumpleaños, Marisol —dice ella, y ambas nos reímos—. Sigo esperando por mi visa, pero utilicé parte del dinero que me enviaste para comprar mi primera computadora y obtener una conexión de internet. Ahora podremos hablar y cantar juntas, y podré ver tu cara bonita todo el tiempo.

—¿Vendrá abuelita a mi fiesta? —le pregunto a mami. Esta vez, ella no sonríe.

¿Qué ha cambiado? ¿Cuál es el efecto del cambio?

(A) ¿Vendrá abuelita a mi fiesta? le pregunto a mami. Esta vez, ella no sonríe.

(B) —¿Vendrá abuelita a mi fiesta? le pregunto a mami. Esta vez, ella no sonríe.

(C) —Vendrá abuelita a mi fiesta —le pregunto a mami. Esta vez, ella no sonríe.

8.2 Los paréntesis

Estándar Usar los paréntesis para incluir información extra.

Frase de enfoque Los paréntesis me ayudan a agregar información.

Invitación a notar Una vez Tío ganó un juego de béisbol por darle una paleta al bateador (¡justo en el momento en que le lanzaban la pelota!).
—Carmen Tafolla, *¿Qué puedes hacer con una paleta?*

Power Note *This sentence not only uses parentheses but also exclamation points (*signos de admiración*). Ask students to visualize the moment in this sentence. Read the sentence with and without the information enclosed in the parentheses. Ask students, "¿Cómo cambia la oración cuando agregas la información en los paréntesis?"*

Invitación a comparar Una vez Tío ganó un juego de béisbol por darle una paleta al bateador (¡justo en el momento en que le lanzaban la pelota!).

Una vez encontré $20 tirado en el suelo (justo en el momento en que quería comprar algo de comer).

Power Note *Ask students, "¿Qué efecto tienen los paréntesis cuando leo en voz alta? ¿Qué efecto tienen cuando leo solamente con mis ojos?"*

Invitación a imitar *Imitate Independently:* Students use the model sentences to create their own sentences, using parentheses to add information.

Invitación a celebrar Students share their sentences aloud, reading them twice.

Invitación a aplicar Students return to a piece of writing to see if there is a moment in which they could add in information using parentheses to give the reader more information about why that moment might be important.

Invitación a corregir

¿Qué aprendimos de Carmen Tafolla acerca de la escritura?	
Una vez Tío ganó un juego de béisbol por darle una paleta al bateador (¡justo en el momento en que le lanzaban la pelota!).	
¿Qué ha cambiado? ¿Cuál es el efecto del cambio?	
(A) Una vez Tío ganó un juego de béisbol por darle una paleta al bateador.	*La información acerca de cuándo ocurrió este momento no está escrita. El lector no sabe que el tío afectó el partido por distraer al bateador.*
(B) Una vez Tío ganó un juego de béisbol por darle una paleta al bateador (justo en el momento en que le lanzaban la pelota).	*Los signos de exclamación no aparecen dentro de los paréntesis. El lector no va a entender la emoción del momento.*
(C) Una vez tío ganó un juego de béisbol por darle una paleta al bateador (¡justo en el momento en que le lanzaban la pelota!).	*Tío está escrito con una letra minúscula. La autora usa* Tío *como si fuera su nombre y necesita una letra mayúscula.*

¿Qué notas?

Una vez Tío ganó un juego de béisbol por darle una paleta al bateador (¡justo en el momento en que le lanzaban la pelota!).

—Carmen Tafolla, *¿Qué puedes hacer con una paleta?*

¿En qué se parecen? ¿En qué se diferencian?

Una vez Tío ganó un juego de béisbol por darle una paleta al bateador (¡justo en el momento en que le lanzaban la pelota!).

Una vez encontré $20 tirado en el suelo (justo en el momento en que quería comprar algo de comer).

Inténtalo

Una vez Tío ganó un juego de béisbol por darle una paleta al bateador (¡justo en el momento en que le lanzaban la pelota!).

Una vez encontré $20 tirado en el suelo (justo en el momento en que quería comprar algo de comer).

Una vez Tío ganó un juego de béisbol por darle una paleta al bateador (¡justo en el momento en que le lanzaban la pelota!).

¿Qué ha cambiado? ¿Cuál es el efecto del cambio?

(A) Una vez Tío ganó un juego de béisbol por darle una paleta al bateador.

(B) Una vez Tío ganó un juego de béisbol por darle una paleta al bateador (justo en el momento en que le lanzaban la pelota).

(C) Una vez tío ganó un juego de béisbol por darle una paleta al bateador (¡justo en el momento en que le lanzaban la pelota!).

9

What Do Adjectives Do?

¿Cuál es la función de los adjetivos?

Writers use adjective to narrow the field from everything to something in particular. It's easy to spew abstract terms when explaining grammar. But telling primary or intermediate writers to add adjectives to *narrow* or *limit* a noun would only confuse them. Even saying, "Adjectives describe" is abstract. It may be true that adjectives describe, but how does that nugget of information delineate adjectives from any other part of speech? Doesn't all language describe? Don't specific nouns and verbs give pictures to our readers as well?

To communicate the precise function of a part of speech in a way that makes sense, we show young writers what adjectives do in writing and reading. The best way to show adjectives at work is to read a text that uses them, so we lift a few sentences with adjectives for students to study. If children don't see adjectives, we rewrite the sentences without them, asking, "What changed?" Students compare and contrast the original version containing adjectives with the revised version without them. This helps young writers see what adjectives do.

Lesson Sets:

9.1 Los adjetivos contestan preguntas

9.2 Los adjetivos después de los sustantivos

9.3 Los adjetivos comparativos

9.4 Los adjetivos superlativos

Correlating English lessons for this chapter can be found in *Patterns of Power*, Chapter 5.

9.1 Los adjetivos contestan preguntas

Estándar Usar y entender los adjetivos.

Frase de enfoque Uso los adjetivos para decir de qué tipo.

Invitación a notar Mi voz se volvió tan poderosa que los hombres peligrosos trataron de silenciarme.
—Malala Yousafzai, *El lápiz mágico de Malala*

Power Note *Students may not immediately notice the adjectives in the sentence. Ask students, "¿Cómo era su voz? ¿Cómo eran los hombres?" Emphasize the focus phrase that adjectives describe what kind.*

Figure 9.1
Anchor Chart

Invitación a comparar Mi voz se volvió tan poderosa que los hombres peligrosos trataron de silenciarme.

Las voces unidas de los trabajadores se volvieron tan poderosas que los dueños despiadados no podían seguir tratándolos de manera injusta.

Power Note *In this imitation, we find a few more adjectives than in the original sentence* (unidas, poderosas, despiadados, injusta). *If students are not noticing the adjectives, use questioning:* ¿Cómo eran las voces? ¿Cómo eran los dueños?

Invitación a imitar

Imitate Together: Invite writers to use interactive or shared writing to compose a sentence with you.

> Los niños se volvieron tan inteligentes que una prueba tramposa no los puede engañar.

Imitate Independently: Students use the model to create their own sentence, using adjectives that tell what kind.

Invitación a celebrar

Collect student imitations on a wall chart that has the focus phrase at the top.

Invitación a aplicar

Have student pairs write a sentence about science or math work, using an adjective to tell what kind.

Invitación a corregir

¿Qué aprendimos de Malala Yousafzai acerca de la escritura?	
Mi voz se volvió tan poderosa que los hombres peligrosos trataron de silenciarme.	
¿Qué ha cambiado? ¿Cuál es el efecto del cambio?	
(A) Mi voz se volvió tan fuerte que los hombres peligrosos trataron de silenciarme.	*La palabra* fuerte *reemplazó la palabra* poderosa. *Aunque las dos tienen un significado muy parecido, la palabra* poderosa *tiene un efecto más grande que la palabra* fuerte.
(B) Mi voz se volvió tan poderosa que los hombres trataron de silenciarme.	*El adjectivo que describe a los hombres desapareció. El lector no sabe cómo son los hombres en esta versión.*
(C) Mi voz se volvió tan poderosa que los hombres peligrosos trató de silenciarme.	*El verbo* trató *no concuerda con el sujeto* los hombres. Hombres *es una palabra plural que requiere otra conjugación del verbo.*

¿Qué notas?

Mi voz se volvió tan poderosa que los hombres peligrosos trataron de silenciarme.
—Malala Yousafzai, *El lápiz mágico de Malala*

¿En qué se parecen? ¿En qué se diferencian?

Mi voz se volvió tan poderosa que los hombres peligrosos trataron de silenciarme.

Las voces unidas de los trabajadores se volvieron tan poderosas que los dueños despiadados no podían seguir tratándolos de manera injusta.

Inténtalo

Mi voz se volvió tan poderosa que los hombres peligrosos trataron de silenciarme.

Las voces unidas de los trabajadores se volvieron tan poderosas que los dueños despiadados no podían seguir tratándolos de manera injusta.

Mi voz se volvió tan poderosa que los hombres peligrosos trataron de silenciarme.

¿Qué ha cambiado? ¿Cuál es el efecto del cambio?

(A) Mi voz se volvió tan fuerte que los hombres peligrosos trataron de silenciarme.

(B) Mi voz se volvió tan poderosa que los hombres trataron de silenciarme.

(C) Mi voz se volvió tan poderosa que los hombres peligrosos trató de silenciarme.

9.2 Los adjetivos después de los sustantivos

Estándar Usar y entender los adjetivos.

Frase de enfoque Normalmente, escribo los adjetivos después de los sustantivos para describir cómo son.

Frase de enfoque Tomás tenía que volver a Tejas. Iba a echar de menos este lugar tranquilo, el agua fresca, los libros lisos y relucientes.
—Pat Mora, *Tomás y la señora de la biblioteca*

Power Note *You might find that students are more familiar with* extrañar *than* echar de menos *to express that they miss someone or something. Clarify for students that Spanish gives us many ways to express our feelings and that the two mean the same thing. If students are not immediately noticing the adjectives, ask, "¿Qué tipo de lugar? ¿Qué tipo de agua? ¿Qué tipo de libros?" This questioning will get them to focus on the adjectives. As we look at the order of nouns and adjectives, it's important to discuss with bilingual students how the patterns change in English and Spanish. In English adjectives generally precede nouns, and in Spanish the noun precedes the adjective. But there are exceptions to this pattern in both languages.*

Invitación a comparar Tomás tenía que volver a Tejas. Iba a echar de menos este lugar tranquilo, el agua fresca, los libros lisos y relucientes.

Alex tenía que cambiar de escuela. Iba a extrañar a su maestra favorita, sus amigos juguetones y la biblioteca gigante.

Power Note *In this imitation, we choose to use the standard form of listing three items in a series (separating the first two items with a comma and the second and third with a conjunction). Students may note that the original sentence doesn't follow the expected pattern. Discuss with students why an author might choose to use commas and no conjunctions and the effect it has on how the sentence is read.*

Invitación a imitar *Imitate Together:* Invite writers to use paired writing to compose a sentence using adjectives after nouns.

Imitate Independently: Students use the model to create their own sentence, using adjectives after nouns.

Invitación a celebrar Create a class book either in print or digitally that demonstrates how adjectives work to clarify nouns. In addition to becoming part of the class library, this book can be shared with others outside the classroom. Students might take it home and read it to someone, or the class might share it with a younger classroom, the principal, the librarian, or other school personnel. Allow students to get creative. As a class, pick a theme, topic, or genre.

Invitación a aplicar

Invite students to return to a previous piece of writing to see if they can add in a few adjectives after nouns to be more descriptive.

Invitación a corregir

¿Qué aprendimos de Pat Mora acerca de la escritura?	
Tomás tenía que volver a Tejas. Iba a echar de menos este lugar tranquilo, el agua fresca, los libros lisos y relucientes.	
¿Qué ha cambiado? ¿Cuál es el efecto del cambio?	
(A) Tomás tenía que volver a tejas. Iba a echar de menos este lugar tranquilo, el agua fresca, los libros lisos y relucientes.	*El nombre del estado está escrito con letra minúscula al inicio. Los nombres del estado se escriben con mayúscula para darles importancia.*
(B) Tomás tenía que volver a Tejas. Iba a echar de menos este tranquilo lugar, el agua fresca, los libros lisos y relucientes.	*El adjectivo que describe al lugar viene antes del sustantivo.* Tranquilo *se debe escribir después del sustantivo que describe.*
(C) Tomás tenía que volver a Tejas. Iba a echar de menos este lugar tranquilo, el agua fresca, los libros liso y reluciente.	*Los adjetivos que describen* los libros *no concuerdan en cantidad. La frase* los libros *indica que son más de uno, así que los adjetivos tienen que terminar en s tambien.*

¿Qué notas?

Tomás tenía que volver a Tejas. Iba a echar de menos este lugar tranquilo, el agua fresca, los libros lisos y relucientes.

—Pat Mora, *Tomás y la señora de la biblioteca*

¿En qué se parecen? ¿En qué se diferencian?

Tomás tenía que volver a Tejas. Iba a echar de menos este lugar tranquilo, el agua fresca, los libros lisos y relucientes.

Alex tenía que cambiar de escuela. Iba a extrañar a su maestra favorita, sus amigos juguetones y la biblioteca gigante.

Inténtalo

Tomás tenía que volver a Tejas. Iba a echar de menos este lugar tranquilo, el agua fresca, los libros lisos y relucientes.

Alex tenía que cambiar de escuela. Iba a extrañar a su maestra favorita, sus amigos juguetones y la biblioteca gigante.

Tomás tenía que volver a Tejas. Iba a echar de menos este lugar tranquilo, el agua fresca, los libros lisos y relucientes.

¿Qué ha cambiado? ¿Cuál es el efecto del cambio?

(A) Tomás tenía que volver a tejas. Iba a echar de menos este lugar tranquilo, el agua fresca, los libros lisos y relucientes.

(B) Tomás tenía que volver a Tejas. Iba a echar de menos este tranquilo lugar, el agua fresca, los libros lisos y relucientes.

(C) Tomás tenía que volver a Tejas. Iba a echar de menos este lugar tranquilo, el agua fresca, los libros liso y reluciente.

9.3 Los adjetivos comparativos

Estándar Usar y entender los adjetivos comparativos.

Frase de enfoque Uso *más/menos* + *adjetivo* + *que* para comparar dos cosas.

Invitación a notar Otra vez se encontró con el viejito que le dijo que tenía un segundo consejo aún más valioso que el primero.
—Joe Hayes, *The Day It Snowed Tortillas/El Día Que Nevaron Tortillas: Folktales Told in Spanish and English*

Power Note *If students are not noticing the phrase that compares two things, ask, "¿Qué tiene el viejito? (Un consejo.) ¿Qué están comparando en esta oración? (El consejo de ayer y el consejo de hoy.) ¿Y cómo comparan?" Highlight the pattern where an adjective is surrounded by* más *or* menos *and* que.

Invitación a comparar Otra vez se encontró con el viejito que le dijo que tenía un segundo consejo aún más valioso que el primero.

Encontré en la playa una conchita aún más bonita que la que encontré ayer.

Power Note *Emphasize with students that this pattern is used for comparing just two things and that we have a slightly different pattern to use when there are more than two things being compared.*

Invitación a imitar *Imitate Together:* Invite writers to use shared writing to compose a sentence with you.

Mi nota en lectura es más alta que mi nota en matemáticas.

Imitate Independently: Students use the model to create their own sentence comparing two things.

Invitación a celebrar Have students read aloud their sentences and invite the class to identify the two things that are being compared.

Invitación a aplicar Students can write a review in their reading journal in which they compare two books. They might use phrases like: *más largo que, más interesante que, menos aburrido que, etc.*

Invitación a corregir

¿Qué aprendimos de Joe Hayes acerca de la escritura?	
Otra vez se encontró con el viejito que le dijo que tenía un segundo consejo aún más valioso que el primero.	
¿Qué ha cambiado? ¿Cuál es el efecto del cambio?	
(A) Otra vez se encontró con el viejito que le dijo que tenía un segundo consejo valioso que el primero.	*Sin la palabra* más, *los lectores no saben cómo los dos consejos se comparan y la frase* que el primero *no tiene sentido.*
(B) Otra vez se encontró con el viejito que le dijo que tenía un segundo consejo aún menos valioso que el primero.	Menos *indica que sus consejos no son válidos. Eso cambia por completo lo que quería decir el autor.*
(C) Otra vez se encuentra con el viejito que le dijo que tenía un segundo consejo aún más valioso que el primero.	*Los verbos deben estar en el mismo tiempo. Si el viejito* dijo *algo, entendemos que ya pasó.* Encuentra *está en el tiempo presente y no concuerda con los demás verbos.*

¿Qué notas?

Otra vez se encontró con el viejito que le dijo que tenía un segundo consejo aún más valioso que el primero.

—Joe Hayes, *Day It Snowed Tortillas/El Día Que Nevaron Tortillas : Folktales Told in Spanish and English*

¿En qué se parecen? ¿En qué se diferencian?

Otra vez se encontró con el viejito que le dijo que tenía un segundo consejo aún más valioso que el primero.

Encontré en la playa una conchita aún más bonita que la que encontré ayer.

Inténtalo

Otra vez se encontró con el viejito que le dijo que tenía un segundo consejo aún más valioso que el primero.

Encontré en la playa una conchita aún más bonita que la que encontré ayer.

Otra vez se encontró con el viejito que le dijo que tenía un segundo consejo aún más valioso que el primero.

¿Qué ha cambiado? ¿Cuál es el efecto del cambio?

(A) Otra vez se encontró con el viejito que le dijo que tenía un segundo consejo valioso que el primero.

(B) Otra vez se encontró con el viejito que le dijo que tenía un segundo consejo aún menos valioso que el primero.

(C) Otra vez se encuentra con el viejito que le dijo que tenía un segundo consejo aún más valioso que el primero.

9.4 Los adjetivos superlativos

Estándar Usar y entender los adjetivos superlativos.

Frase de enfoque Uso *el/la* + *más/menos* + adjetivo para expresar algo al máximo.

Invitación a notar A veces, las palabras más sencillas eran las más poderosas.
—Peter H. Reynolds, *El coleccionista de palabras*

Power Note *Remind students that we use the pattern of* article + más/menos + adjective *when we are speaking about more than two things. In this case Reynolds is talking about the simplest of all words being the most powerful of all words.*

Invitación a comparar A veces, las palabras más sencillas eran las más poderosas.

A veces, los poemas más cortos son los más impactantes.

Power Note *Review with students the articles in Spanish* (el/los, la/las) *as they are needed to follow the pattern. Help students notice that in the beginning of each sentence we are using a similar pattern but stating the noun. In the second part of the sentence the noun is implied.*

Invitación a imitar *Imitate Together:* Invite writers to use shared writing to compose a sentence with you.

A veces, los estudiantes más callados son los más pensativos.

Imitate Independently: Students use the model to create their own sentence, using superlatives.

Invitación a celebrar Line up a few well-loved books from your classroom library. Use the pattern to talk about the books. *¿Cuál es el más largo de todos? ¿Cuál es el más corto? ¿Cuál es el más interesante?* It might be hard to come to a consensus on the last question.

Invitación a aplicar Students should return to a narrative piece of writing in their notebooks or writing folders. They should look for a moment when they might be able to add in a superlative adjective phrase. *Era el día más largo de mi* vida . . .

Invitación a corregir

¿Qué aprendimos de Peter H. Reynolds acerca de la escritura?	
A veces, las palabras más sencillas eran las más poderosas.	
¿Qué ha cambiado? ¿Cuál es el efecto del cambio?	
(A) A veces, las palabras más sencillas eran poderosas.	*Se ha quitado la frase* las más *antes de* poderosas. *El significado cambia y no parece que las palabras sencillas son más poderosas que todas las otras palabras.*
(B) A veces, las palabras más sencillas eran la más poderosa.	*La frase* la más poderosa *e refiere a una idea singular. En esta oración,* palabras *es plural y los adjetivos tienen que concordar.*
(C) Las palabras más sencillas eran las más poderosas.	*Sin la frase adverbial* a veces, *parece que las palabras sencillas siempre eran poderosas y eso cambia el sentido de la oración.*

¿Qué notas?

A veces, las palabras más sencillas eran las más poderosas.

—Peter H. Reynolds, *El coleccionista de palabras*

¿En qué se parecen? ¿En qué se diferencian?

A veces, las palabras más sencillas eran las más poderosas.

A veces, los poemas más cortos son los más impactantes.

Inténtalo

A veces, las palabras más sencillas eran las más poderosas.

A veces, los poemas más cortos son los más impactantes.

A veces, las palabras más sencillas eran las más poderosas.

¿Qué ha cambiado? ¿Cuál es el efecto del cambio?

(A) A veces, las palabras más sencillas eran poderosas.

(B) A veces, las palabras más sencillas eran la más poderosa.

(C) Las palabras más sencillas eran las más poderosas.

10

What Do Adverbs Do?

¿Cuál es la función de los adverbios?

Most simply, adverbs do what they say. They add to verbs. Specifically, they add *how*, *where*, and *when* they happen. Writers use adverbs to add clarity and specificity to their verbs.

But, beloved horror writer Stephen King warns, "The road to hell is paved with adverbs." In fact, people say all sorts of nasty things about adverbs. They are maligned as lazy writing. Annie Dillard writes, "Adverbs are a sign that you've used the wrong verb." These kinds of comments make some writers think they should never use an adverb.

Still, writers will call on adverbs frequently and—when applied as an intentional craft move—they can really enhance a piece of writing. The trick is to show young writers that, though adverbs are a great tool to show detail and clarify their writing, a big part of the author's craft is to know when to use them and when to use them sparingly.

Lesson Sets:

10.2 Los adverbios que demuestran cómo

10.2 Los adverbios que demuestran frecuencia

10.3 Los adverbios que demuestran dónde

Correlating English lessons for this chapter can be found in *Patterns of Power*, Chapter 15.

10.1 Los adverbios que demuestran cómo

Estándar Formar y usar los adverbios (¿Cómo?: modo e intensidad).

Frase de enfoque Uso los adverbios para demostrar cómo pasa algo.

Invitación a notar Ahora las parejas interraciales podían casarse legalmente en Virginia.
—Selina Alko, *El caso de Los Loving: La lucha por el matrimonio interracial*

Power Note *If you have already taught* adverbios de tiempo *students will note* ahora *as an adverb in this sentence. Affirm their understanding and reinforce the focus phrase and that we are looking for an adverb that shows* how something *happens.*

Invitación a comparar Ahora las parejas interraciales podían casarse legalmente en Virginia.

En el invierno, las mariposas vuelan libremente en los bosques de Michoacán.

Power Note *Students may note that both sentences start with an adverb or an adverbial phrase. Draw students' attention to* los adverbios de modo (legalmente *and* libremente*) and their placement in the sentences. Ask students to generate a list of adverbs that follow the same pattern (forma feminina del adjetivo + el sufijo* -mente*). Students can use this as they move into the Invitation to Imitate.*

Invitación a imitar As a class, use interactive writing to imitate Alko's sentence to describe how your class does certain routines during the day. Students can practice adding *-mente* to common adjectives to then describe the verbs in sentences. Here are some examples:

> Nos ponemos en fila silenciosamente.
>
> Nos lavamos las manos rápidamente después de ir al baño.

Figure 10.1
Fourth graders experiment with adverbs

En el otoño las hojas se caen lentamente.

Mi hermanito pidio una patineta urgentemente.

Invitación a aplicar

The Actors' Workshop: Working from a class-generated list of words that end in *-mente,* invite students to write out commands that can be performed in the classroom *(Cierra la puerta fuertemente o cierra la puerta suavemente)* and act them out. Post the list titled *Adverbios de modo* in the classroom. You can extend this list by providing the antonym for the adverbs that students originally llisted (*ligeramente/fuertemente, cuidadosamente/peligrosamente,* etc.) and act those out, too.

Invitación a corregir

¿Qué aprendimos de Selina Alko acerca de la escritura?	
Ahora las parejas interraciales podían casarse legalmente en Virginia.	
¿Qué ha cambiado? ¿Cuál es el efecto del cambio?	
(A) Ahora las parejas interraciales podían casarse legal en Virginia.	Legal es *un adjetivo aunque aquí necesitamos un adverbio para describir* cómo se *podían casar. Usamos adjetivos para describir los sustantivos.*
(B) Ahora las parejas interraciales podían casarse en Virginia legalmente.	Legalmente *está ubicada al final de la oración. Mover el adverbio después de* Viriginia *enfatiza que la ley ha cambiado en ese estado específico.*
(C) Ahora las parejas interraciales podían casarse legalmente en virginia.	Virginia *empieza con la letra minúscula. Sabemos que los nombres de los estados llevan mayúscula inicial.*

¿Qué notas?

Ahora las parejas interraciales podían casarse legalmente en Virginia.

—Selina Alko, *El caso de Los Loving: La lucha por el matrimonio interracial*

¿En qué se parecen? ¿En qué se diferencian?

Ahora las parejas interraciales podían casarse legalmente en Virginia.

En el invierno, las mariposas vuelan libremente en los bosques de Michoacán.

Inténtalo

Ahora las parejas interraciales podían casarse legalmente en Virginia.

En el invierno, las mariposas vuelan libremente en los bosques de Michoacán.

Ahora las parejas interraciales podían casarse legalmente en Virginia.

¿Qué ha cambiado? ¿Cuál es el efecto del cambio?

(A) Ahora las parejas interraciales podían casarse legal en Virginia.

(B) Ahora las parejas interraciales podían casarse en Virginia legalmente.

(C) Ahora las parejas interraciales podían casarse legalmente en virginia.

10.2 Los adverbios que demuestran frecuencia

Estándar Usar los adverbios para modificar los verbos, indicando frecuencia.

Frase de enfoque Uso los adverbios para demostrar cuándo pasa algo.

Invitación a notar El calor siempre ha sido mi amigo. Siempre lo he querido.
— Amado Peña y Juanita Alba, *Calor: A Story of Warmth for All Ages*

Power Note *The word* siempre *is telling when something happens. In this case,* siempre *goes along with* ser *and* querer *in this example.*

Invitación a comparar El calor siempre ha sido mi amigo. Siempre lo he querido.

El sol nunca ha sido mi amigo. A veces me deja quemado.

Power Note *If students are having a hard time noticing the adverbs, try isolating the predicate of the sentence and asking,* ¿Con qué frecuencia pasa eso? *In the second sentence of the imitation the words* a veces *function as one idea and, in this case, the adverb.*

Invitación a imitar *Imitate Together:* Use shared or interactive writing to imitate the sentences. You might try out several adverbs of time to tell when something happened or will happen.

Imitate Independently: Generate with students a list of adverbs that indicate time. Title this chart *Adverbios de tiempo*. Include words like: *ahora, antes, después, siempre, nunca, pronto, tarde, hoy, ayer, mañana, aun, todavía, ya,* etc. Have students use this chart to create their own sentence or sentences.

Invitación a aplicar *Playtime: ¿Cuál es la palabra de* cuándo? Throughout the day have students look and listen for time words. Discuss how time words give us a way to show when something happened, happens, or will happen. Model possibilities: *Hoy vamos a correr antes de ir a la cafetería. Acabo de usar un adverbio de tiempo. ¿Qué palabra fue?* Repeat the sentence as necessary. Have a student keep a tally of all the adverbs of time they find throughout the day.

Invitación a corregir

¿Qué aprendimos de Amado Peña y Juanita Alba acerca de la escritura?	
El calor siempre ha sido mi amigo. Siempre lo he querido.	
¿Qué ha cambiado? ¿Cuál es el efecto del cambio?	
(A) El calor ha sido mi amigo. Lo he querido.	*Sin los adverbios, el lector no tiene idea del tiempo y falta la intensidad de las oraciones originales.*
(B) El calor nunca ha sido mi amigo. Nunca lo he querido.	*El adverbio* nunca *cambia el sentido de las oraciones. Ahora, parece que al narrador no le gusta el calor.*
(C) El calor ha sido mi amigo hoy. Lo quiero.	*El adverbio* hoy *cambia el tiempo con que el narrador ha querido el calor. Parece que este sentimiento ha durado solamente un día.*

¿Qué notas?

El calor siempre ha sido mi amigo. Siempre lo he querido.

— Amado Peña y Juanita Alba, *Calor: A Story of Warmth for All Ages*

¿En qué se parecen? ¿En qué se diferencian?

El calor siempre ha sido mi amigo. Siempre lo he querido.

El sol nunca ha sido mi amigo. A veces me deja quemado.

Inténtalo

El calor siempre ha sido mi amigo. Siempre lo he querido.

El sol nunca ha sido mi amigo. A veces me deja quemado.

El calor siempre ha sido mi amigo. Siempre lo he querido.

¿Qué ha cambiado? ¿Cuál es el efecto del cambio?

(A) El calor ha sido mi amigo. Lo he querido.

(A) El calor nunca ha sido mi amigo. Nunca lo he querido.

(A) El calor ha sido mi amigo hoy. Lo quiero.

10.3 Los adverbios que demuestran dónde

Estándar Usar los adverbios para demostrar *dónde*.

Frase de enfoque Uso los adverbios para demostrar *dónde* pasa algo.

Invitación a notar Después de terminar mi tarea mi mamá me deja jugar afuera.
—Duncan Tonatiuh, *Querido Primo*

Power Note *If you have already taught adverbs of time, students might immediately notice* después. *Draw their attention to the word* afuera *by asking students, "¿Dónde le deja jugar?" Then bring in the focus phrase to show that adverbs are not just for describing how or when, but also where.*

Invitación a comparar Después de terminar mi tarea mi mamá me deja jugar afuera.

Después de aprender a montar bien mi bicicleta, mi mamá me dejó dar vueltas alrededor del vecindario.

Power Note *Remind students that adverbs can answer the question, "¿Dónde?" When you focus students' attention to place or position, they will notice* alrededor. *Begin generating a class list of* adverbios de lugar. *Start with the most basic:* aquí, allá, afuera, adentro, cerca, lejos, *etc.*

Invitación a imitar *Imitate Together:* Refer to the chart you have begun with students listing adverbs of place. Invite students to use shared writing to compose a sentence with you. Choose your adverb of place before getting started.

> Después de hacer mis quehaceres, mi mamá me dejó caminar al parque cerca de la casa.

Imitate Independently: Have students refer to the chart of adverbios de lugar to craft a sentence.

Invitación a celebrar After a student shares his/her sentences aloud, listeners raise their hands and pick out the place word in the sentence. The class agrees by standing up or sitting down. Add any place words to the chart that are not already on there as you hear them in the sentences.

Invitación a aplicar Students reread something they've written and see if they need to show where something happened. They may also add other adverbs that show how or when something happened.

Invitación a corregir

¿Qué aprendimos de Amado Peña y Juanita Alba acerca de la escritura?	
Después de terminar mi tarea mi mamá me deja jugar afuera.	
¿Qué ha cambiado? ¿Cuál es el efecto del cambio?	
(A) Mi mamá me deja jugar afuera.	*Sin el adverbio* después *y la frase que sigue, el lector no sabe cuándo la mamá lo deja jugar.*
(B) Después de terminar mi tarea mi mamá me deja jugar.	*Sin el adverbio* afuera, *no es claro dónde va a jugar.*
(C) Después de terminar mi tarea mi Mamá me deja jugar afuera.	*En este caso,* mamá *no se usa como nombre propio. Cuando* mi *precede* mamá, *no vamos a usar una letra mayúscula.*

¿Qué notas?

Después de terminar mi tarea mi mamá me deja jugar afuera.

—Duncan Tonatiuh, *Querido Primo*

¿En qué se parecen? ¿En qué se diferencian?

Después de terminar mi tarea mi mamá me deja jugar afuera.

Después de aprender a montar bien mi bicicleta, mi mamá me dejó dar vueltas alrededor del vecindario.

Inténtalo

Después de terminar a mi tarea mi mamá me deja jugar afuera.

Después de aprender a montar bien mi bicicleta, mi mamá me dejó dar vueltas alrededor del vecindario.

Después de terminar mi tarea mi mamá me deja jugar afuera.

¿Qué ha cambiado? ¿Cuál es el efecto del cambio?

(A) Mi mamá me deja jugar afuera.

(B) Después de terminar mi tarea mi mamá me deja jugar.

(C) Después de terminar mi tarea mi Mamá me deja jugar afuera.

11

What Do Prepositions Do?

¿Cuál es la función de las preposiciones?

Prepositions are far more than *anywhere a cat can go*, and the long-term goal is for students to understand that prepositions help writers add detail to their writing, answering readers' questions of *where* and *when*, grounding readers in space and time.

You may recall that adverbs do this too—tell where and when. But the subtle difference is that ***adverbs add to verbs***, and ***prepositions show relationships between nouns*** and other parts of speech. Two of the most common prepositions in Spanish also happen to be the only two contractions in Spanish. You'll find that lesson here with the other prepopsitions. (Check out Chapter 9 in *Patterns of Power* if you are looking for a contractions lesson in English.)

The words that follow a preposition (including a noun or nouns) make a prepositional phrase (a group of words that follow a preposition). Prepositional phrases tell the location of characters and objects and the relationships between them. They also show the relationship of events in the space of time. A writer can anticipate a listener or reader's questions of where and when with prepositional phrases: *Before school*, I had breakfast *in the cafeteria*.

Lesson Sets:

Correlating English lessons for this chapter can be found in *Patterns of Power*, Chapter 16.

11.1 Las preposiciones de *dónde*

Estándar Usar y entender las preposiciones y las frases preposicionales.

Frase de enfoque Uso las preposiciones para expresar *dónde*.

Invitación a notar Un día, en la madrugada, mi tía Toya escuchó desde su cama un ritmo de palmas que provenía de la cocina del comedor.
—Jorge Argueta, *La fiesta de las tortillas*

Power Note *Try giving students a version of the sentence without the prepositional phrases that indicate* where. Un día, en la madrugada, mi tía Toya escuchó un ritmo. *Add the prepositional phrases that tell* where *back into the sentence and discuss the effect.*

Invitación a comparar Un día, en la madrugada, mi tía Toya escuchó desde su cama un ritmo de palmas que provenía de la cocina del comedor.

En la mañana, escuché desde mi casa el gruñido y silbido del autobús en la calle. Entonces, supe que perdí el autobus.

Power Note *In this imitation, we hear a prepositional phrase telling where the narrator is and a prepositional phrase that tells where the bus is. If students are pointing out the other prepositional phrase* (en la mañana)*, affirm that they have found another prepositional phrase and that soon you will continue your investigation into prepositional phrases of* cuándo.

Invitación a imitar *Imitate Together:* Invite writers to use interactive or shared writing to compose a sentence with you. Here is an example:

> Escuchamos desde la puerta la risa de mi abuela viendo sus telenovelas en su cuarto.

Imitate Independently: Students use model sentences to compose their own imitations, using prepositional phrases to show where things are.

Invitación a celebrar For a new celebration, we learn the lyrics to a preposition song in Spanish. You'll find several by searching YouTube. A class favorite is called "Las preposiciones" and has a baby dancing in sunglasses. Having a list memorized will help young writers intentionally use prepositions to give their reader more information. The goal of teaching prepositions is to give students another way to integrate details into their writing.

Invitación a aplicar Students can meet with a learning buddy one or two grade levels below them to teach them the prepositions song. With their buddies, they can generate sentences that use prepositional phrases.

Invitación a corregir

¿Qué aprendimos de Jorge Argueta acerca de la escritura?	
Un día, en la madrugada, mi tía Toya escuchó desde su cama un ritmo de palmas que provenía de la cocina del comedor.	
¿Qué ha cambiado? ¿Cuál es el efecto del cambio?	
(A) Mi tía Toya escuchó desde su cama un ritmo de palmas que provenía de la cocina del comedor.	*No hay información en esta oración indicando cuándo ocurrió este momento. El lector sabe que ya pasó porque los verbos usan el tiempo del pasado, pero sin la frase* un día, en la madrugada *no sabemos cuándo pasó esto.*
(B) Un día, en la madrugada, mi tía Toya escuchó un ritmo de palmas.	*Sin las frases preposicionales, el lector no sabe dónde estaba la tía o de dónde venía el sonido. Las frases preposicionales dan más información al lector.*
(C) Un día, en la madrugada, mi Tía Toya escuchó desde su cama un ritmo de palmas que provenía de la cocina del comedor.	*No es necesario usar la letra mayúscula en la palabra* tía. *Su nombre lleva letra mayúscula, pero solamente usamos una letra mayúscula en* tía *si lo estamos usando como su nombre.*

¿Qué notas?

Un día, en la madrugada, mi tía Toya escuchó desde su cama un ritmo de palmas que provenía de la cocina del comedor.

—Jorge Argueta, *La fiesta de las tortillas*

¿En qué se parecen? ¿En qué se diferencian?

Un día, en la madrugada, mi tía Toya escuchó desde su cama un ritmo de palmas que provenía de la cocina del comedor.

En la mañana, escuché desde mi casa el gruñido y silbido del autobús en la calle. Entonces, supe que perdí el autobus.

Inténtalo

Un día, en la madrugada, mi tía Toya escuchó desde su cama un ritmo de palmas que provenía de la cocina del comedor.

En la mañana, escuché desde mi casa el gruñido y silbido del autobús en la calle. Entonces, supe que perdí el autobus.

Un día, en la madrugada, mi tía Toya escuchó desde su cama un ritmo de palmas que provenía de la cocina del comedor.

¿Qué ha cambiado? ¿Cuál es el efecto del cambio?

(A) Mi tía Toya escuchó desde su cama un ritmo de palmas que provenía de la cocina del comedor.

(B) Un día, en la madrugada, mi tía Toya escuchó un ritmo de palmas.

(C) Un día, en la madrugada, mi Tía Toya escuchó desde su cama un ritmo de palmas que provenía de la cocina del comedor.

11.2 Las preposiciones de *cuándo*

Estándar Usar y entender las preposiciones y las frases preposicionales.

Frase de enfoque Uso las preposiciones para expresar *cuándo.*

Invitación a notar En el invierno, está bajo y tranquilo. En el verano, está lleno y ruidoso.
—Maya Christina González, *Yo sé que el río me ama*

Power Note *The prepositional phrases in these sentences are* en el invierno *and* en el verano. *If students do not notice the prepositional phrases during this invitation, try reading the sentences without the prepositional phrases. Students will then notice that the phrases indicate* when.

Invitación a comparar En el invierno, está bajo y tranquilo. En el verano, está lleno y ruidoso.

Mis estudiantes están despiertos y listos en la mañana. En la tarde, están cansados y distraídos.

Power Note *In this imitation, we switch up the placement of the prepositional phrases. This helps the students notice that prepositional prhases can appear in multiple places in a sentence.*

Invitación a imitar *Imitate Together:* Invite writers to use interactive or shared writing to compose a sentence with you.

Durante la clase de escritura, compartimos nuestras historias.

Imitate Independently: Students use the model sentences from the Invitation to Compare as well as others created by the class to compose their own imitation.

Invitación a aplicar Invite students to contribute to a class chart by logging what happens during the regular school day. Challenge them not to always use the same preposition. Collect other prepositions that explain when, such as *después, hasta, durante, antes*, etc.

Invitación a corregir

¿Qué aprendimos de Maya Christina Gonzalez acerca de la escritura?	
En el invierno, está bajo y tranquilo. En el verano, está lleno y ruidoso.	
¿Qué ha cambiado? ¿Cuál es el efecto del cambio?	
(A) En el Invierno, está bajo y tranquilo. En el Verano, está lleno y ruidoso.	*Los nombres de las estaciones están escritos con mayúscula. Los nombres de las estaciones no llevan mayúscula inicial.*
(B) Al invierno, está bajo y tranquilo. Al verano, está lleno y ruidoso.	*La preposición aquí cambió. La preposición al se usa frecuentemente en los destinos y direcciones. La mejor preposición para las estaciones del año es en.*
(C) En el invierno, está bajo o tranquilo. En el verano, está lleno o ruidoso.	*La conjunción ha cambiado a o. Los adjetivos describen el río en estas temporadas. Por eso, y es la mejor conjunción para juntar los dos adjetivos.*

¿Qué notas?

En el invierno, está bajo y tranquilo. En el verano, está lleno y ruidoso.

—Maya Christina González, *Yo sé que el río me ama*

¿En qué se parecen? ¿En qué se diferencian?

En el invierno, está bajo y tranquilo. En el verano, está lleno y ruidoso.

Mis estudiantes están despiertos y listos en la mañana. En la tarde, están cansados y distraídos.

Inténtalo

En el invierno, está bajo y tranquilo. En el verano, está lleno y ruidoso.

Mis estudiantes están despiertos y listos en la mañana. En la tarde, están cansados y distraídos.

En el invierno, está bajo y tranquilo. En el verano, está lleno y ruidoso.

¿Qué ha cambiado? ¿Cuál es el efecto del cambio?

(A) En el Invierno, está bajo y tranquilo. En el Verano, está lleno y ruidoso.

(B) Al invierno, está bajo y tranquilo. Al verano, está lleno y ruidoso.

(C) En el invierno, está bajo o tranquilo. En el verano, está lleno o ruidoso.

11.3 Las contracciones *del* y *al*

Estándar Usar y entender las contracciones *del* y *al*.

Frase de enfoque Uso *del* en vez de *de el*. Uso *al* en vez de *a el*.

Invitación a notar Cuando éramos niños, mi mamá y mi abuela se enojaban con nosotros cuando jugábamos bajo el sol caliente del mediodía. Nos decían que éramos como los camaleones al mediodía que juegan sin importarles nada.
—Carmen Lomas Garza, *En mi familia*

Power Note *Students might notice many aspects of these sentences: accents, complex sentences, or verb tense. Ask students to focus in on the phrases* del mediodía *and* al mediodía. *In the phrase* bajo el sol caliente, *try following it with* del verano *or* de la primavera. *Ask if letters have been squeezed out to make the words flow when we read them aloud. Remind bilingual students that we have many contractions in English but only two in Spanish.*

Invitación a comparar Cuando éramos niños, mi mamá y mi abuela se enojaban con nosotros cuando jugábamos bajo el sol caliente del mediodía. Nos decían que éramos como los camaleones al mediodía que juegan sin importarles nada.

Yo estoy detrás de él, de puntitas, pues no quiero que se me suban las hormigas.

Power Note *Consider reading the excerpt "*Los camaleones*" from* En mi familia *to students. Lomas Garza's pictures and words work together to create vivid imagery in the reader's mind. In this invitation we choose to look at a phrase, where we would not create a contraction in Spanish. Compare the phrases* del mediodía *(which is equivalent to* de el mediodía*) to* de él. *We collapse the words into one when the article* el *follows* de *or* a. *We do not collapse the words into one when the pronoun* él *follows the preposition.*

Invitación a imitar *Imitate Together:* Invite writers to use interactive or shared writing to compose a sentence with you. Here is an example:

> Mi mamá se enoja mucho si juego afuera sin mi chaqueta con el aire frío del invierno.

Imitate Independently: Students use model sentences to compose their own imitations, using the contractions *del* or *al*.

Invitación a celebrar Have students narrate their school day. *Vamos al parque. Es la foto del maestro de música.* Act like you are squeezing out letters with the palms of your hands when you hear the two contractions.

Invitación a aplicar Students look through a writing journal or folder and consider adding in *del* or *al* phrases to add more information for their readers.

Invitación a corregir

¿Qué aprendimos de Carmen Lomas Garza acerca de la escritura?	
Cuando éramos niños, mi mamá y mi abuela se enojaban con nosotros cuando jugábamos bajo el sol caliente del mediodía. Nos decían que éramos como los camaleones al mediodía que juegan sin importarles nada.	
¿Qué ha cambiado? ¿Cuál es el efecto del cambio?	
(A) Cuando éramos niños, mi mamá y mi abuela se enojaban con nosotros cuando jugábamos bajo el sol caliente de el mediodía. Nos decían que éramos como los camaleones a el mediodía que juegan sin importarles nada.	*Las frases* de el *y* a el *no fluyen al leerlas en voz alta. Como se repiten los sonidos de los vocales, se lee con más fluidez si usamos* del *y* al.
(B) Cuando éramos niños, mi Mamá y mi Abuela se enojaban con nosotros cuando jugábamos bajo el sol caliente del mediodía. Nos decían que éramos como los camaleones al mediodía que juegan sin importarles nada.	*En esta oración* mamá *y* abuela *no se usan como sus nombres. Sabemos eso por los pronombres posesivos antes de los sustantivos. No es necesario usar la letra mayúscula en este caso.*
(C) Cuando éramos niños, mi mamá y mi abuela se enojan con nosotros cuando jugábamos bajo el sol caliente del mediodía. Nos decían que éramos como los camaleones al mediodía que juegan sin importarles nada.	*El tiempo de los verbos cambió con el verbo* enojan. *Mantenemos los verbos en el pasado porque la autora está hablando de cuando era niña. Es confuso para el lector si cambiamos el tiempo de los verbos sin razón.*

¿Qué notas?

Cuando éramos niños, mi mamá y mi abuela se enojaban con nosotros cuando jugábamos bajo el sol caliente del mediodía. Nos decían que éramos como los camaleones al mediodía que juegan sin importarles nada.

—Carmen Lomas Garza, *En mi familia*

¿En qué se parecen? ¿En qué se diferencian?

Cuando éramos niños, mi mamá y mi abuela se enojaban con nosotros cuando jugábamos bajo el sol caliente del mediodía. Nos decían que éramos como los camaleones al mediodía que juegan sin importarles nada.

Yo estoy atrás de él, de puntitas, pues no quiero que se me suban las hormigas.

Inténtalo

Cuando éramos niños, mi mamá y mi abuela se enojaban con nosotros cuando jugábamos bajo el sol caliente del mediodía. Nos decían que éramos como los camaleones al mediodía que juegan sin importarles nada.

Yo estoy atrás de él, de puntitas, pues no quiero que se me suban las hormigas.

Cuando éramos niños, mi mamá y mi abuela se enojaban con nosotros cuando jugábamos bajo el sol caliente del mediodía. Nos decían que éramos como los camaleones al mediodía que juegan sin importarles nada.

¿Qué ha cambiado? ¿Cuál es el efecto del cambio?

(A) Cuando éramos niños, mi mamá y mi abuela se enojaban con nosotros cuando jugábamos bajo el sol caliente de el mediodía. Nos decían que éramos como los camaleones a el mediodía que juegan sin importarles nada.

(B) Cuando éramos niños, mi Mamá y mi Abuela se enojaban con nosotros cuando jugábamos bajo el sol caliente del mediodía. Nos decían que éramos como los camaleones al mediodía que juegan sin importarles nada.

(C) Cuando éramos niños, mi mamá y mi abuela se enojan con nosotros cuando jugábamos bajo el sol caliente del mediodía. Nos decían que éramos como los camaleones al mediodía que juegan sin importarles nada.

12

What Do Conjunctions Do?

¿Cuál es la función de las conjunciones?

onjunctions are like doors that lead into another room—a passageway or link to other words, sentence parts and sentences.

The prefix *con-* in ***con**junction* is a variant of the prefix *com-*, meaning "together" or "with." And ***junction*** means "the act of joining or combining." That's what conjunctions do—combine and join things together. Conjunctions are tools writers use to create effects that enhance the meaning of their message. They can join equal words, phrases, clauses, or sentences.

In the following lessons, we look specifically at coordinating conjunctions—using *y* to combine, *o* to show options, or *Ni . . . ni* to show negative correlations.

Lesson Sets:

12.1 La conjunción *y*

12.2 Uso de la *o* para mostrar alternativas

12.3 Ni . . . ni

Correlating English lessons for this chapter can be found in *Patterns of Power*, Chapter 17.

12.1 La conjunción *y*

Estándar Usar las conjunciones.

Frase de enfoque Uso la *y* para unir dos cosas.

Invitación a notar

Power Note *For a different* ***Invitación a notar****, read aloud* Rosita y Conchita *by Eric Gonzalez and Erick Haeger. Ask students to summarize the main events in the story. The conversation might go like this:*

—¿Qué pasó en este cuento?—dices.
—Conchita y Rosita se encuentran en el Día de los Muertos.
—Así es —dices—. Una manera que podemos unir dos nombres está escrito en el título.
—Rosita y Conchita—dicen los estudiantes.
—Exacto —dices—. Y une dos nombres.

Invitación a comparar Rosita y Conchita

Juan y el chupacabras

Clara y la curandera

Power Note *We choose to use titles instead of sentences in this comparison to call students' attention to all the signals and craft that titles provide. For fun, students may want to generate other pairs. If students begin to list three or more things you may decide to move forward with a discussion of lists or save that lesson for later.*

Invitación a imitar *Imitate Together:* Invite writers to use interactive, shared, or paired writing to compose a sentence with you. Brainstorm as many pairs as possible from the world around us.

Espagueti y albóndigas

Jairo y Génesis

Hamburguesas y papas fritas

Imitate independently: Students use the model to create their own pair, using the coordinating conjunction *y*. They can illustrate their pair if they want.

Invitación a celebrar Create a wall chart and title it *El poder de la* Y. Post kids' work all over the chart. As students continue to find pairs in reading in other subject areas or in their own writing they can add those to the chart as well.

Invitación a aplicar Hunt for the use of y throughout the day and talk about its function of putting things together.

12.2 Uso de la *o* para mostrar alternativas

Estándar Usar las conjunciones.

Frase de enfoque Uso la *o* para mostrar las alternativas.

Invitación a notar Madre Cielo mira a su alrededor, pero Nochecita no está asomada detrás de los montes, o escondida dentro de las cuevas, u oculta entre los campos.
—Yuyi Morales, *Nochecita*

Power Note *This sentence from Yuyi Morales lets us see the function of* o *as well as the way it changes based on the word that follows. Read aloud what would happen if* o *did not change to* u*. Students may say that you cannot hear* o *if it comes right before* oculta*. Students may also notice that there are three ideas separated by commas. Though it is unnecessary for the author to use* o *before the second idea and a comma between the second and third, this will bring up a discussion of author's craft.*

Invitación a comparar Madre Cielo mira a su alrededor, pero Nochecita no está asomada detrás de los montes, o escondida dentro de las cuevas, u oculta entre los campos.

Busqué a mi hermano por todos lados, pero no estaba acostado debajo de la cama, escondido detrás de las cortinas u oculto en la ropa del closet.

Power Note *In this imitation, we follow the conventional pattern for lists by not repeating* o *and removing the last comma.*

Invitación a imitar *Imitate Together:* Invite writers to use paired writing to compose a sentence using *o*.

Imitate Independently: Students use the model to compose their own sentences using the conjunction *o* to show options or alternatives.

Invitación a celebrar Students share their sentences with the class, reading them twice. Clap for every writer to create an audience and a community that recognizes the hard work of writing.

Invitación a aplicar Students generate sentences in which they present three choices of what they would like to get or do as a reward in the class.

Invitación a corregir

¿Qué aprendimos de Yuyi Morales acerca de la escritura?	
Madre Cielo mira a su alrededor, pero Nochecita no está asomada detrás de los montes, o escondida dentro de las cuevas, u oculta entre los campos.	
¿Qué ha cambiado? ¿Cuál es el efecto del cambio?	
(A) Madre Cielo mira a su alrededor, pero Nochecita no está asomada detrás de los montes, y escondida dentro de las cuevas, y oculta entre los campos.	*La conjunción* y *no presenta los lugares posibles como opciones. Es confuso para el lector porque la oración indica que Madre Cielo no encuentra a Nochecita en ninguno de estos lugares.*
(B) Madre Cielo mira a su alrededor pero Nochecita no está asomada detrás de los montes, o escondida dentro de las cuevas, u oculta entre los campos.	*No hay una coma antes de la palabra pero. Esta es una oración compuesta con la conjunción* pero *y, por eso, requiere una coma.*
(C) Madre Cielo mira a su alrededor, pero Nochecita no está asomada detrás de los montes, o escondida dentro de las cuevas, o oculta entre los campos.	*La conjunción* o *aparece justamente antes de una palabra que empieza con la* o. *Tenemos que usar* u *para diferenciar entre la palabra* o *y la palabra* oculta.

¿Qué notas?

Madre Cielo mira a su alrededor, pero Nochecita no está asomada detrás de los montes, o escondida dentro de las cuevas, u oculta entre los campos.

—Yuyi Morales, *Nochecita*

¿En qué se parecen? ¿En qué se diferencian?

Madre Cielo mira a su alrededor, pero Nochecita no está asomada detrás de los montes, o escondida dentro de las cuevas, u oculta entre los campos.

Busqué a mi hermano por todos lados, pero no estaba acostado debajo de la cama, escondido detrás de las cortinas u oculto en la ropa del closet.

Inténtalo

Madre Cielo mira a su alrededor, pero Nochecita no está asomada detrás de los montes, o escondida dentro de las cuevas, u oculta entre los campos.

Busqué a mi hermano por todos lados, pero no estaba acostado debajo de la cama, escondido detrás de las cortinas u oculto en la ropa del closet.

Madre Cielo mira a su alrededor, pero Nochecita no está asomada detrás de los montes, o escondida dentro de las cuevas, u oculta entre los campos.

¿Qué ha cambiado? ¿Cuál es el efecto del cambio?

(A) Madre Cielo mira a su alrededor, pero Nochecita no está asomada detrás de los montes, y escondida dentro de las cuevas, y oculta entre los campos.

(B) Madre Cielo mira a su alrededor pero Nochecita no está asomada detrás de los montes, o escondida dentro de las cuevas, u oculta entre los campos.

(C) Madre Cielo mira a su alrededor, pero Nochecita no está asomada detrás de los montes, o escondida dentro de las cuevas, o oculta entre los campos.

12.3 Ni . . . ni

Estándar Usar las conjunciones.

Frase de enfoque Uso *ni* para expresar dos cosas que no describen lo que quiero decir.

Invitación a notar Desgraciadamente, no me siento ni de aquí, ni de allá. Ni suficientemente mexicana. Ni suficientemente americana.
—Raquel Valle Sentíes, del poema "Soy como soy y qué" en *Cool Salsa*

Power Note *These sentences offer a nice opportunity to review adverbs, but focus students' attention on the use of* ni. *Ask students, "¿Qué quiere decir la autora con estas frases? ¿Cómo lo sabes?" Emphasize that* ni *always goes along with pairs. You might acknowledge for students that the last two phrases are not complete sentences. Ask why an author might have decided to separate these phrases as if they were sentences.*

Invitación a comparar Desgraciadamente, no me siento ni de aquí, ni de allá. Ni suficientemente mexicana. Ni suficientemente americana.

En el campo del fútbol, no me siento ni torpe, ni Messi. Ni suficientemente bueno para que me pasen la pelota. Ni tan descoordinado para que me corran del partido.

Power Note *Discuss what the word* ni *does in each of the sentences. Remind students that* ni *works for pairs of ideas.*

Invitación a imitar *Imitate Together:* Invite writers to help you write a sentence using ni to describe a pair of things that didn't happen or don't describe what you want to say.

Invitación a corregir

¿Qué aprendimos de Raquel Valle Sentíes acerca de la escritura?	
Desgraciadamente, no me siento ni de aquí, ni de allá.	
¿Qué ha cambiado? ¿Cuál es el efecto del cambio?	
(A) Desgraciadamente, no me siento de aquí y de allá.	*La conjunción* y *no expresa que la narradora no se siente conectada con ningún lugar.*
(B) Desgraciadamente, no me siento ni de aquí, o de allá.	*Usamos* ni *con pares de cosas, así que no es suficiente usar* ni *solamente una vez.*
(C) Desgraciada, no me siento ni de aquí, ni de allá.	*Usar el adjetivo* desgraciada *en vez del adverbio* desgraciadamente *deja al lector con la duda sobre qué está diciendo la narradora.*

¿Qué notas?

Desgraciadamente, no me siento ni de aquí, ni de allá. Ni suficientemente mexicana. Ni suficientemente americana.

—Raquel Valle Sentíes, del poema "Soy como soy y qué" en *Cool Salsa*

¿En qué se parecen? ¿En qué se diferencian?

Desgraciadamente, no me siento ni de aquí, ni de allá. Ni suficientemente mexicana. Ni suficientemente americana.

En el campo del fútbol, no me siento ni torpe, ni Messi. Ni suficientemente bueno para que me pasen la pelota. Ni tan descoordinado para que me corran del partido.

Inténtalo

Desgraciadamente, no me siento ni de aquí, ni de allá. Ni suficientemente mexicana. Ni suficientemente americana.

En el campo del fútbol, no me siento ni torpe, ni Messi. Ni suficientemente bueno para que me pasen la pelota. Ni tan descoordinado para que me corran del partido.

Desgraciadamente, no me siento ni de aquí, ni de allá.

¿Qué ha cambiado? ¿Cuál es el efecto del cambio?

(A) Desgraciadamente, no me siento de aquí y de allá.

(B) Desgraciadamente, no me siento ni de aquí, o de allá.

(C) Desgraciada, no me siento ni de aquí, ni de allá.

13

Why Do Writers Use Compound Sentences?

¿Por qué los escritores usan las oraciones compuestas?

Compound sentences are made when two or more sentences are joined together with a coordinating conjunction. The joined sentences each have their own subject and verb.

In Spanish compound sentences using *las conjunciones copulativas* do not require a comma (though we can find exceptions to this pattern). However, compound sentences that use *las conjunciones adversativas* do require a comma. Because this is different from patterns in English, it is important to give students many opportunities to notice when authors use commas and when they don't.

If your writers are finding difficulty identifying what qualities it takes to make a sentence (a subject and a conjugated verb), take a few lessons to shore this up with them. Students will need a notion of what makes a sentence before we can successfully invite them into exploring how two or more sentences can be joined together.

Lesson Sets

13.1 Combinar oraciones con *y*

13.2 Combinar oraciones con *y* o *pero*

13.3 Combinar oraciones con *sino que*

Correlating English lessons for this chapter can be found in *Patterns of Power*, Chapter 18.

13.1 Combinar oraciones con *y*

Estándar Usar una conjunción coordinante para formular una oración compuesta.

Frase de enfoque Uso *y* para unir dos oraciones simples para formar una oración compuesta.

Invitación a notar día 1 Puso un espejo sobre su cama.

Frida empezó a pintar retratos de su cara, una y otra vez.

Power Note *Because compound sentences are two simple sentences combined, we separate this invitation into two days. Go through the normal noticings, honoring, naming and extending. At the end of the exploration, ask students if they believe the two sentences to be related. Show students the picture of Frida Kahlo's wooden canopy bed (see Figure 13.1). Have students work in pairs to see if they can come up with how to put the ideas together to make one sentence. Students should share their ideas.*

Invitación a notar día 2 Puso un espejo sobre su cama y Frida empezó a pintar retratos de su cara, una y otra vez.
—Alma Flor Ada, *Caminos*

Power Note *Say, "Este es el patrón que la autora Alma Flor Ada usó. Vamos a explorar lo que podemos notar en la oración de Ada." Go through the sentence test for each side of the compound sentence. Ask for each part, "¿Quién o qué hace algo? ¿Qué hizo o qué es?"*

Invitación a comparar Puso un espejo sobre su cama y Frida empezó a pintar retratos de su cara, una y otra vez.

Me senté en la mesa y mi mamá me obligó a practicar las tablas de multiplicar, una y otra vez.

Power Note *Point out to students that the phrases on either side of the conjunction represent complete sentences. It is essential that students understand* los sujetos tácitos *to be able to identify each phrase as its own simple sentence. Repeat this compound sentence test with every compound sentence you examine. It's that important.*

Invitación a imitar *Imitate Together:* Invite writers to use interactive paired writing to compose a compound sentence using the conjunction *y*.

Imitate Independently: Students use the model to create their own sentences, using the coordinating conjuction *y* to combine two sentences.

Invitación a celebrar

Volunteers read their imitation sentences aloud. This is the best celebration of all—having an audience for which writers can write.

Invitación a aplicar

With a partner, writers compose a compound sentence about a character's feelings in a book they're reading. Partners should ensure that there is a complete simple sentence on either side of the conjuction.

Invitación a corregir

¿Qué aprendimos de Alma Flor Ada acerca de la escritura?	
Puso un espejo sobre su cama y Frida empezó a pintar retratos de su cara, una y otra vez.	
¿Qué ha cambiado? ¿Cuál es el efecto del cambio?	
(A) Puso un espejo sobre su cama Frida empezó a pintar retratos de su cara, una y otra vez.	*Se ha quitado la conjunción. Ahora tenemos una oración sin puntuación. Tenemos que usar una conjunción o punto y seguido.*
(B) Puso un espejo sobre su cama, y Frida empezó a pintar retratos de su cara, una y otra vez.	*En español no es necesario usar una coma antes de una conjunción coordinante como y o e. Es posible encontrar excepciones si un autor quiere más separación entre las dos ideas.*
(C) Puso un espejo sobre su cama y Frida empieza a pintar retratos de su cara, una y otra vez.	*El tiempo de los verbos cambió. La primera parte de la oración ocurrió en el pasado y la segunda parte debe usar el tiempo pasado también.*

Figure 13.1
Frida's Bed en la Casa Azul in Coyoacán, México City

¿Qué notas?

Puso un espejo sobre su cama y Frida empezó a pintar retratos de su cara, una y otra vez.

—Alma Flor Ada, *Caminos*

¿En qué se parecen? ¿En qué se diferencian?

Puso un espejo sobre su cama y Frida empezó a pintar retratos de su cara, una y otra vez.

Me senté en la mesa y mi mamá me obligó a practicar las tablas de multiplicar, una y otra vez.

Inténtalo

Puso un espejo sobre su cama y Frida empezó a pintar retratos de su cara, una y otra vez.

Me senté en la mesa y mi mamá me obligó a practicar las tablas de multiplicar, una y otra vez.

Puso un espejo sobre su cama y Frida empezó a pintar retratos de su cara, una y otra vez.

¿Qué ha cambiado? ¿Cuál es el efecto del cambio?

(A) Puso un espejo sobre su cama Frida empezó a pintar retratos de su cara, una y otra vez.

(B) Puso un espejo sobre su cama, y Frida empezó a pintar retratos de su cara, una y otra vez.

(C) Puso un espejo sobre su cama y Frida empieza a pintar retratos de su cara, una y otra vez.

13.2 Combinar oraciones con *y* o *pero*

Estándar Usar una conjunción coordinante copulativa o una coma y una conjunción coordinante adversativa para formular una oración compuesta.

Frase de enfoque Uso una coma y *pero* para unir dos oraciones simples y formar una oración compuesta.

Invitación a notar día 1 Mi mamá quiso sembrar el terreno, pero el dueño le dijo que no. Buscó trabajo, pero en todos lados le pagaban muy poquito. . . . Así, un día, mi mamá puso sus cosas en una bolsa, nos tomó de la mano y dejamos nuestra casa.
—José Manuel Mateo, *Migrar*

Power Note *For this two-day invitation we look at two examples of compound sentences using a comma and* pero. *Students may notice a series of actions separated by a comma and* y. *Affirm their thinking, but return to the two compound sentences to do the compound sentence test: Cover the conjunction and check that each side of the sentence could form it's own simple sentence.*

Invitación a notar día 2 Llegamos en camión hasta las vías del tren y ahí esperamos. . . . El tren nunca se detuvo y tuvimos que subirnos al vuelo. Casi me quedo, pero mi hermana alcanzó a jalarme. Un señor chaparrito también me empujó para ayudarme, pero él no alcanzó a subir. Correr no fue divertido esa vez.
—José Manuel Mateo y Javier Martínez Pedro, *Migrar*

Power Note *In this excerpt we find two different patterns of compound sentences. In Spanish compound sentences using* las conjunciones copulativas *do not require a comma (though we can find exceptions to this pattern). However, compound sentences that use* las conjunciones adversativas *do require a comma. Because this is different from patterns in English, it is important to give students many opportunities to notice when authors use commas and when they don't. Begin a chart of compound sentences in Spanish, separating sentences that are generally separated by a comma and sentences that aren't.*

Invitación a comparar El tren nunca se detuvo y tuvimos que subirnos al vuelo.

El tren nunca se detuvo, pero tuvimos que subir de todos modos.

Power Note *In this invitation we take just one sentence from the original excerpts. The comparison sentence expresses essentially the same idea in a slightly different format. We want to focus in on the different ways to combine sentences in Spanish.*

Invitación a imitar

Imitate Together: Invite writers to use interactive paired writing to compose a compound sentence using the conjunction *pero*.

Imitate in Pairs: Students use the model to create their own sentences, one compound sentence using *y* and one compound sentence using *pero*.

Invitación a celebrar

Pairs read aloud their sentences saying the word *coma* to indicate when a comma is used. The listeners should affirm if they agree with the placement of the comma.

Invitación a aplicar

At the end of each subject throughout the day students should write a compound sentence to summarize learning.

Invitación a corregir

¿Qué aprendimos de José Manuel Mateo acerca de la escritura?	
El tren nunca se detuvo y tuvimos que subirnos al vuelo. Casi me quedo, pero mi hermana alcanzó a jalarme. Un señor chaparrito también me empujó para ayudarme, pero él no alcanzó a subir.	
¿Qué ha cambiado? ¿Cuál es el efecto del cambio?	
(A) El tren nunca se detuvo, y tuvimos que subirnos al vuelo. Casi me quedo, pero mi hermana alcanzó a jalarme. Un señor chaparrito también me empujó para ayudarme, pero él no alcanzó a subir.	*Hay una coma antes de y en la primera oración. Esa coma no es necesaria.*
(B) El tren nunca se detuvo y tuvimos que subirnos al vuelo. Casi me quedo pero mi hermana alcanzó a jalarme. Un señor chaparrito también me empujó para ayudarme pero él no alcanzó a subir.	*Se han quitado las comas antes de pero en dos oraciones. Es necesario usar las comas porque las ideas presentadas en las oraciones expresan algo contrario a la primera idea.*
(C) El tren nunca se detuvo. Tuvimos que subirnos al vuelo. Casi me quedo. Mi hermana alcanzó a jalarme. Un señor chaparrito también me empujó para ayudarme. Él no alcanzó a subir.	*Todas las oraciones son oraciones simples. Al leerlas en voz alta suenan entrecortadas.*

¿Qué notas?

[Day 1]

Mi mamá quiso sembrar el terreno, pero el dueño le dijo que no. Buscó trabajo, pero en todos lados le pagaban muy poquito. . . . Así, un día, mi mamá puso sus cosas en una bolsa, nos tomó de la mano y dejamos nuestra casa.
—José Manuel Mateo, *Migrar*

[Day 2]

Llegamos en camión hasta las vías del tren y ahí esperamos. . . . El tren nunca se detuvo y tuvimos que subirnos al vuelo. Casi me quedo, pero mi hermana alcanzó a jalarme. Un señor chaparrito también me empujó para ayudarme, pero él no alcanzó a subir. Correr no fue divertido esa vez.
—José Manuel Mateo y Javier Martínez Pedro, *Migrar*

¿En qué se parecen? ¿En qué se diferencian?

El tren nunca se detuvo y tuvimos que subirnos al vuelo.

El tren nunca se detuvo, pero tuvimos que subir de todos modos.

Inténtalo

El tren nunca se detuvo y tuvimos que subirnos al vuelo.

El tren nunca se detuvo, pero tuvimos que subir de todos modos.

El tren nunca se detuvo y tuvimos que subirnos al vuelo. Casi me quedo, pero mi hermana alcanzó a jalarme. Un señor chaparrito también me empujó para ayudarme, pero él no alcanzó a subir.

¿Qué ha cambiado? ¿Cuál es el efecto del cambio?

(A) El tren nunca se detuvo, y tuvimos que subirnos al vuelo. Casi me quedo, pero mi hermana alcanzó a jalarme. Un señor chaparrito también me empujó para ayudarme, pero él no alcanzó a subir.

(B) El tren nunca se detuvo y tuvimos que subirnos al vuelo. Casi me quedo pero mi hermana alcanzó a jalarme. Un señor chaparrito también me empujó para ayudarme pero él no alcanzó a subir.

(C) El tren nunca se detuvo. Tuvimos que subirnos al vuelo. Casi me quedo. Mi hermana alcanzó a jalarme. Un señor chaparrito también me empujó para ayudarme. Él no alcanzó a subir.

13.3 Combinar oraciones con *sino que*

Estándar Usar una coma y una conjunción adversativa para formular una oración compuesta.

Frase de enfoque Uso una coma y *sino que* para unir dos oraciones simples para formar una oración compuesta.

Invitación a notar En ese momento descubrió que no sólo había olvidado la dirección de Diana, sino que también había olvidado el regalo.
—Diane Gonzales Bertrand, *De cabeza y al revés*

Power Note *Review the construction of the compound sentence with students. Remind them that they must pay close attention in Spanish to when the comma is required. Add* sino que *to a list of* conjugaciones adversativas.

Figure 13.3
Anchor chart to keep track of when to use a comma.

Invitación a comparar

En ese momento descubrió que no sólo había olvidado la dirección de Diana, sino que también había olvidado el regalo.

En ese momento se dio cuenta de que no sólo había olvidado su tarea, sino que también había olvidado su bolsa de almuerzo.

Power Note *As students notice how the sentences are alike and different, continue to repeat the focus phrase:* Uso una coma y *sino que* para unir dos oraciones simples para crear una oración compuesta.

Invitación a imitar

Imitate Together: Invite writers to use interactive or shared writing to compose a sentence with you.

> No solo tenía que limpiar la cocina, sino que tenía que aspirar toda la casa.

Imitate Independently: Students use the model to create their own sentences using a comma and *sino que* to join two ideas.

Invitación a celebrar

Students share their *sino que* compound sentence aloud, saying the word *coma* to indicate when a comma is used.

Invitación a aplicar

Students write a *sino que* sentence to describe a concept in math, science, or social studies.

Invitación a corregir

¿Qué aprendimos de Diane Gonzales Bertrand acerca de la escritura?	
En ese momento descubrió que no sólo había olvidado la dirección de Diana, sino que también había olvidado el regalo.	
¿Qué ha cambiado? ¿Cuál es el efecto del cambio?	
(A) En ese momento descubrió que no sólo había olvidado la dirección de Diana sino que también había olvidado el regalo.	*Falta la coma antes de* sino que. *Las conjunciones adversativas requieren una coma para separar las dos partes de la oración compuesta.*
(B) En ese momento descubrió que no sólo había olvidado la dirección de Diana. También había olvidado el regalo.	*Son dos oraciones simples. Sin la conjunción, dos ideas que están conectadas se muestran separadas.*
(C) En ese momento descubrió que no sólo había olvidado la dirección de Diana y también había olvidado el regalo.	*La conjunción* y *une dos ideas. Sin embargo,* y *no cumple la misma función de enfatizar que había olvidado la dirección a la vez que se le olvidó el regalo.*

¿Qué notas?

En ese momento descubrió que no sólo había olvidado la dirección de Diana, sino que también había olvidado el regalo.

—Diane Gonzales Bertrand, *De cabeza y al revés*

¿En qué se parecen? ¿En qué se diferencian?

En ese momento descubrió que no sólo había olvidado la dirección de Diana, sino que también había olvidado el regalo.

En ese momento se dio cuenta de que no sólo había olvidado su tarea, sino que también había olvidado su bolsa de almuerzo.

Inténtalo

En ese momento descubrió que no sólo había olvidado la dirección de Diana, sino que también había olvidado el regalo.

En ese momento se dio cuenta de que no sólo había olvidado su tarea, sino que también había olvidado su bolsa de almuerzo.

En ese momento descubrió que no sólo había olvidado la dirección de Diana, sino que también había olvidado el regalo.

¿Qué ha cambiado? ¿Cuál es el efecto del cambio?

(A) En ese momento descubrió que no sólo había olvidado la dirección de Diana sino que también había olvidado el regalo.

(B) En ese momento descubrió que no sólo había olvidado la dirección de Diana. También había olvidado el regalo.

(C) En ese momento descubrió que no sólo había olvidado la dirección de Diana y también había olvidado el regalo.

14

Why Do Writers Use the Serial Comma?

¿Por qué los escritores usan la coma en una serie?

Ah, the simplicity of the serial comma.

When we are children, lists are one of the first ways we learn to combine things—things to buy when we're shopping, things to do or remember. We don't have to ask for only one thing for breakfast or have only one reason to be able to get a dog. A pair is nice, but when we have three or more, only the serial or list comma will do.

Lists are a way to pack specific nouns and examples into one sentence. Lists give writers a way to link actions. Yes, authors separate the items in the list, but the whole purpose of the comma is to both separate and connect. Punctuation talks to the reader.

A period says, "Stop."

A comma says, "But wait, there's more."

Lesson Sets:

14.1 La coma serial para separar ideas en una lista

14.2 La coma serial para separar una lista de sustantivos

14.3 La coma serial para separar acciones en una lista

Correlating English lessons for this chapter can be found in *Patterns of Power*, Chapter 19.

14.1 La coma serial para separar ideas en una lista

Estándar Usar una coma y una conjunción en una serie.

Frase de enfoque Uso una coma y una conjunción para separar tres ideas acciones en una lista.

Invitación a notar Los niños sujetan sus libros, se despiden y regresan a sus casas.
—Jeanette Winter, *Biblioburro: Una historia real de Colombia*

Power Note *You can find several clips online featuring Luis Soriano who brings books to children in rural areas of Colombia. You might show just a short clip so students can visualize the moment referenced in the Invitation to Notice. Once students notice a comma in this sentence, have them collaborate with their table groups on what they believe the comma is doing when they read this sentence aloud and when they read it with our eyes. Share out their theories.*

Invitación a comparar Los niños sujetan sus libros, se despiden y regresan a sus casas.

Luis Soriano les trae libros de fantasía, misterio e información.

Power Note *In the Invitation to Notice, we find a list of verbs. In the Invitation to Compare we use a list of nouns. We do this to show that we can use this pattern with nouns, adjectives or verbs.*

Figure 14.1a
Anchor chart for commas in a series

Invitación a imitar

Imitate Together: Invite writers to use interactive or shared writing to compose a sentence with you.

> Los estudiantes empacan sus mochilas, se despiden del maestro y se van a sus casas.

Imitate Independently: Students use the model sentences to create their own sentences, using a comma and conjunction to separate words in a list—choosing to use adjectives, nouns, or verbs.

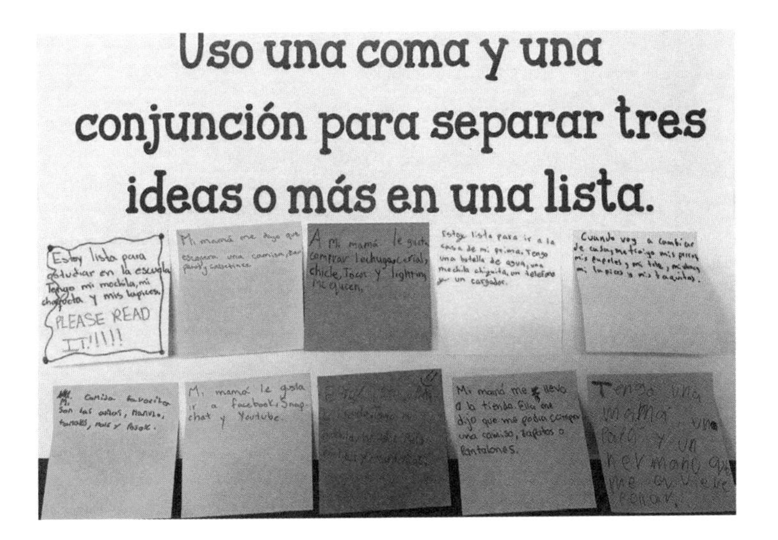

Figure 14.1b
Collecting imitations below the focus phrase

Invitación a celebrar

Students share their sentences with classmates by reading them aloud or sharing them online. Celebrating is sharing with an audience, large or small. Sometimes we may only share with a partner or table group, but sharing is crucial.

Invitación a corregir

¿Qué aprendimos de Jeanette Winter acerca de la escritura?	
Los niños sujetan sus libros, se despiden y regresan a sus casas.	
¿Qué ha cambiado? ¿Cuál es el efecto del cambio?	
(A) Los niños sujetan sus libros se despiden y regresan a sus casas.	*No hay una coma entre* libros *y* se despiden. *Acuérdense de que usamos la coma para separar 3 cosas o más en una lista. Si no la usamos, es confuso para el lector.*
(B) Los niños sujetan sus libros, se despiden, regresan a sus casas.	*La conjunción ha sido omitida. La oración fluye mejor al leerla en voz alta cuando tiene la palabra* y *entre la segunda y tercera idea.*
(C) Los niños sujetan sus libros, se despiden y regresaban a sus casas.	*Los verbos no concuerdan con el tiempo.* Regresaban *indica que ocurrió en el pasado, mientras que* sujetan *y* se despiden *indican el tiempo presente. Cuando los verbos cambian de tiempo es confuso para el lector.*

¿Qué notas?

Los niños sujetan sus libros, se despiden y regresan a sus casas.

—Jeanette Winter, *Biblioburro: Una historia real de Colombia*

¿En qué se parecen? ¿En qué se diferencian?

Los niños sujetan sus libros, se despiden y regresan a sus casas.

Luis Soriano les trae libros de fantasía, misterio e información.

Inténtalo

Los niños sujetan sus libros, se despiden y regresan a sus casas.

Luis Soriano les trae libros de fantasía, misterio e información.

Los niños sujetos sus libros, se despiden y regresan a sus casas.

¿Qué ha cambiado? ¿Cuál es el efecto del cambio?

(A) Los niños sujetan sus libros se despiden y regresan a sus casas.

(B) Los niños sujetan sus libros, se despiden, regresan a sus casas.

(C) Los niños sujetan sus libros, se despiden y regresaban a sus casas.

14.2 La coma serial para separar una lista de sustantivos

Estándar Usar una coma y una conjunción en una serie.

Frase de enfoque Uso una coma y una conjunción para separar tres cosas en una lista.

Invitación a notar Estoy lista para mi paseo en bicicleta. Llevo mis largas bermudas azules, mi casco rojo y una camiseta blanca colgando hasta las rodillas.
—Lori Marie Carlson, "Me gusta montar mi bicicleta" *de Sol a sol*

Power Note *This list of nouns gives the reader a clear picture of what the narrator is wearing as she sets off to ride her bike. Ask students, "¿Qué hacen la coma y la conjunción en esta oración?" Give students a chance to build a theory about what the comma and conjunction do when they read the sentence aloud and when they read it silently. If they need support, you might prompt them by asking, "¿Cuántas cosas constiuyen una lista? ¿Cuáles son las cosas de una lista en esta oración? ¿Cómo lo saben?"*

Invitación a comparar Estoy lista para mi paseo en bicicleta. Llevo mis largas bermudas azules, mi casco rojo y una camiseta blanca colgando hasta las rodillas.

Estoy listo para escribir mi propio libro. Tengo lápices, marcadores, papel y miles de ideas.

Power Note *In this lesson we are focusing on nouns in a list, so ask them to think about the things they see and touch when they're getting ready to do something at home.*

Invitación a imitar *Imitate Independently:* Students write their own sentences, using a comma(s) and conjunction to separate and connect at least three things they touch or see as they get ready to do something.

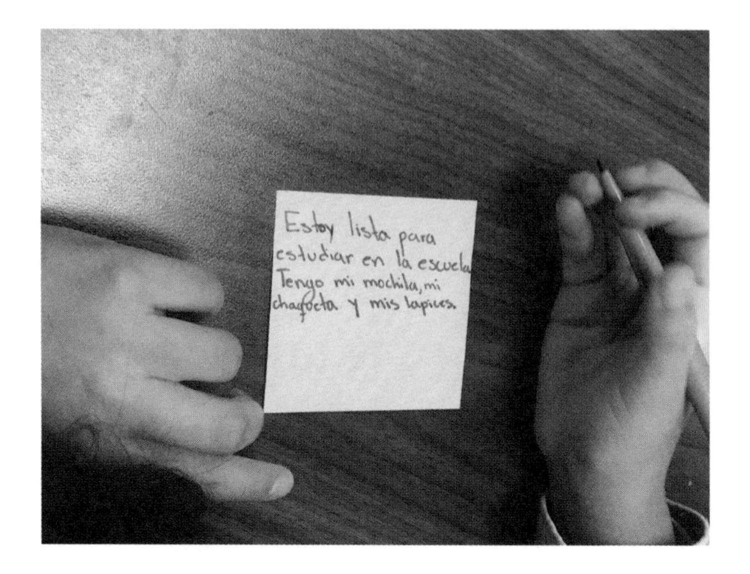

Figure 14.2a
A fourth grader practices generating a list of ideas with a comma and conjunction

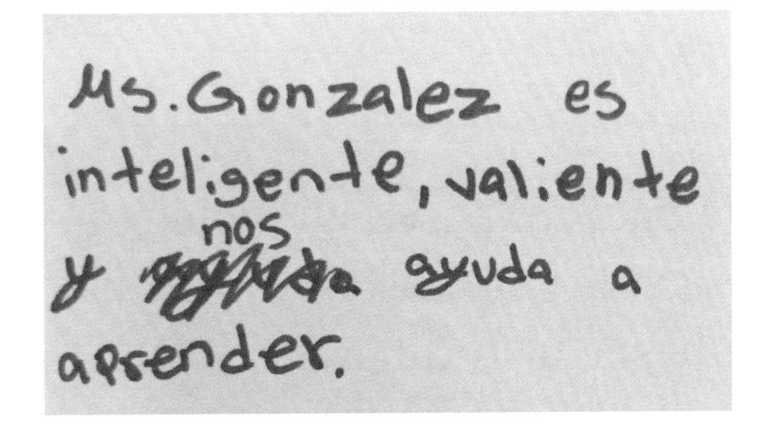

Figure 14.2b
Student describes her teacher using a list

Invitación a celebrar

Students share their sentences saying the word *coma* for emphasis when they have one in their sentence, even though we don't typically read that way.

Invitación a aplicar

Have students return to a piece of writing and find a place where they can describe what someone was wearing by writing items in a list.

Invitación a corregir

¿Qué aprendimos de Lori Marie Carlson acerca de la escritura?	
Estoy lista para mi paseo en bicicleta. Llevo mis largas bermudas azules, mi casco rojo y una camiseta blanca colgando hasta las rodillas.	
¿Qué ha cambiado? ¿Cuál es el efecto del cambio?	
(A) Estoy lista para mi paseo en bicicleta. Llevo mis largas bermudas azules mi casco rojo y una camiseta blanca colgando hasta las rodillas.	*No hay una coma entre la idea de las bermudas y el casco. Acuérdense de que usamos la coma para separar 3 cosas o más en una lista. Si no la usamos, es confuso para el lector.*
(B) Estoy lista para mi paseo en bicicleta. Llevo mis bermudas, mi casco y una camiseta.	*Los adjetivos ya no están describiendo los sustantivos. Pregunta,* ¿Cuál es el efecto de quitar los adjetivos?
(C) Estaba lista para mi paseo en bicicleta. Llevo mis largas bermudas azules, mi casco rojo y una camiseta blanca colgando hasta las rodillas.	*Los verbos no concuerdan con el tiempo.* Estaba *indica que ocurrió en el pasado, mientras que* llevo *indica el tiempo presente. Cuando los verbos cambian de tiempo, es confuso para el lector.*

¿Qué notas?

Estoy lista para mi paseo en bicicleta. Llevo mis largas bermudas azules, mi casco rojo y una camiseta blanca colgando hasta las rodillas.

—Lori Marie Carlson, "Me gusta montar mi bicicleta" de *Sol a sol*

¿En qué se parecen? ¿En qué se diferencian?

Estoy lista para mi paseo en bicicleta. Llevo mis largas bermudas azules, mi casco rojo y una camiseta blanca colgando hasta las rodillas.

Estoy listo para escribir mi propio libro. Tengo lápices, marcadores, papel y miles de ideas.

Inténtalo

Estoy lista para mi paseo en bicicleta. Llevo mis largas bermudas azules, mi casco rojo y una camiseta blanca colgando hasta las rodillas.

Estoy listo para escribir mi propio libro. Tengo lápices, marcadores, papel y miles de ideas.

Estoy lista para mi paseo en bicicleta. Llevo mis largas bermudas azules, mi casco rojo y una camiseta blanca colgando hasta las rodillas.

¿Qué ha cambiado? ¿Cuál es el efecto del cambio?

(A) Estoy lista para mi paseo en bicicleta. Llevo mis largas bermudas azules mi casco rojo y una camiseta blanca colgando hasta las rodillas.

(B) Estoy lista para mi paseo en bicicleta. Llevo mis bermudas, mi casco y una camiseta.

(C) Estaba lista para mi paseo en bicicleta. Llevo mis largas bermudas azules, mi casco rojo y una camiseta blanca colgando hasta las rodillas.

14.3 La coma serial para separar acciones en una lista

Estándar Usar una coma y una conjunción en una serie.

Frase de enfoque Uso una coma y una conjunción para separar tres o más acciones en una lista.

Invitación a notar Todo está silencioso cuando mi mamá entra en el alto edificio de oficinas de vidrio donde ella friega los azulejos de los baños hasta que brillan como la luna, limpia las ventanas altas de cristal hasta ponerlas tan claras como el lago donde mi papá me enseñó a nadar, y limpia y les da brillo a los pisos hasta que quedan tan lisos que podrías deslizarte por ellos si te quitaras los zapatos.
—Diana Cohn, *¡Sí, Se Puede! Yes, We Can! Janitor Strike in L.A.*

Power Note *This sentence does use a comma before the conjunction* y *to set off the last item in this series. It is not customary in Spanish to use a comma before the conjunction* y *for items in a series or compound sentences. However, in Diana Cohn's sentence, the three items in the list include so much detail that the final comma helps the reader understand what the three ideas in the list are.*

Invitación a comparar Todo está silencioso cuando mi mamá entra en el alto edificio de oficinas de vidrio donde ella friega los azulejos de los baños hasta que brillan como la luna, limpia las ventanas altas de cristal hasta ponerlas tan claras como el lago donde mi papá me enseñó a nadar, y limpia y les da brillo a los pisos hasta que quedan tan lisos que podrías deslizarte por ellos si te quitaras los zapatos.

Cuando mi abuela hace tortillas a mano, muele los granos de elote en su licuadora hasta que forma una fina arena dorada, amasa la bola de masa como si estuviera muy enojada con ella, y la aplasta con todo su fuerza en la tortilladora.

Power Note *In this invitation, we choose to use the conventional pattern of not putting a comma before the conjunction between the last two ideas to show students how authors make intentional craft decisions.*

Invitación a imitar *Imitate Together:* Invite writers to use interactive or shared writing to compose a sentence with you.

> Armando escribió un cuento, lo leyó en el micrófono enfrente de todos nosotros y aplaudimos como nunca antes porque era el cuento más bonito que habíamos escuchado.

Imitate Independently: Students use the model sentences to create their own sentences, using a comma and conjunction to separate three ideas in a list.

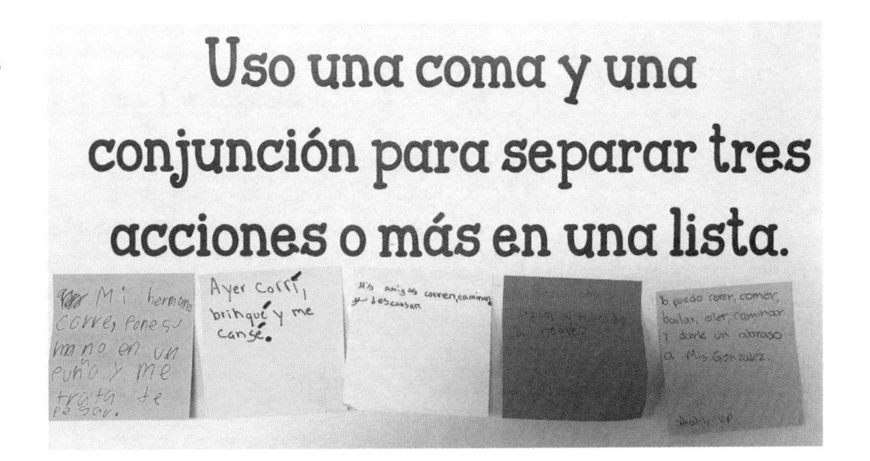

Figure 14.3
Collecting imitations below the focus phrase

Invitación a celebrar

Sometimes the experimenting is the celebration. Celebrate as students are trying new things, sharing, and succeeding.

Invitación a corregir

¿Qué aprendimos de Diana Cohn acerca de la escritura?	
Todo está silencioso cuando mi mamá entra en el alto edificio de oficinas de vidrio donde ella friega los azulejos de los baños hasta que brillan como la luna, limpia las ventanas altas de cristal hasta ponerlas tan claras como el lago donde mi papá me enseñó a nadar, y limpia y les da brillo a los pisos hasta que quedan tan lisos que podrías deslizarte por ellos si te quitaras los zapatos.	
¿Qué ha cambiado? ¿Cuál es el efecto del cambio?	
(A) Todo está silencioso cuando mi mamá entra en el alto edificio de oficinas de vidrio donde ella friega los azulejos de los baños hasta que brillan como la luna limpia las ventanas altas de cristal hasta ponerlas tan claras como el lago donde mi papá me enseñó a nadar, y limpia y les da brillo a los pisos hasta que quedan tan lisos que podrías deslizarte por ellos si te quitaras los zapatos.	*No hay una coma entre* luna *y* limpia. *Es confuso para el lector no separar las ideas. El lector no sabe dónde tomar una pausa.*
(B) Todo estaba silencioso cuando mi mamá entra en el alto edificio de oficinas de vidrio donde ella friega los azulejos de los baños hasta que brillan como la luna, limpia las ventanas altas de cristal hasta ponerlas tan claras como el lago donde mi papá me enseñó a nadar, y limpia y les da brillo a los pisos hasta que quedan tan lisos que podrías deslizarte por ellos si te quitaras los zapatos.	*Los verbos no concuerdan en el tiempo.* Estaba *está escrito en el tiempo pasado y* entra *en el tiempo presente. Se deben evitar diferentes tiempos verbales dentro de una misma oración.*
(C) Todo está silencioso cuando mi mamá entra en el alto edificio de oficinas de vidrio donde ella friega los azulejos de los baños, limpia las ventanas altas de cristal hasta ponerlas claras, y limpia y les da brillo a los pisos hasta que quedan lisos.	*Las frase descriptivas ya no están. Aunque el significado de la oración no ha cambiado, faltan las frases que ayudan al lector a visualizar el trabajo de la mamá.*

¿Qué notas?

Todo está silencioso cuando mi mamá entra en el alto edificio de oficinas de vidrio donde ella friega los azulejos de los baños hasta que brillan como la luna, limpia las ventanas altas de cristal hasta ponerlas tan claras como el lago donde mi papá me enseñó a nadar, y limpia y les da brillo a los pisos hasta que quedan tan lisos que podrías deslizarte por ellos si te quitaras los zapatos.
—Diana Cohn, ¡Sí, Se Puede! *Yes, We Can! Janitor Strike in L.A.*

¿En qué se parecen? ¿En qué se diferencian?

Todo está silencioso cuando mi mamá entra en el alto edificio de oficinas de vidrio donde ella friega los azulejos de los baños hasta que brillan como la luna, limpia las ventanas altas de cristal hasta ponerlas tan claras como el lago donde mi papá me enseñó a nadar, y limpia y les da brillo a los pisos hasta que quedan tan lisos que podrías deslizarte por ellos si te quitaras los zapatos.

Cuando mi abuela hace tortillas a mano, muele los granos de elote en su licuadora hasta que forma una fina arena dorada, amasa la bola de masa como si estuviera muy enojada con ella, y la aplasta con todo su fuerza en la tortilladora.

Inténtalo

Todo está silencioso cuando mi mamá entra en el alto edificio de oficinas de vidrio donde ella friega los azulejos de los baños hasta que brillan como la luna, limpia las ventanas altas de cristal hasta ponerlas tan claras como el lago donde mi papá me enseñó a nadar, y limpia y les da brillo a los pisos hasta que quedan tan lisos que podrías deslizarte por ellos si te quitaras los zapatos.

Cuando mi abuela hace tortillas a mano, muele los granos de elote en su liquadora hasta que forma una fina arena dorada, amasa la bola de masa como si estuviera muy enojada con ella, y la aplasta con todo su fuerza en la tortilladora.

Todo está silencioso cuando mi mamá entra en el alto edificio de oficinas de vidrio donde ella friega los azulejos de los baños hasta que brillan como la luna, limpia las ventanas altas de cristal hasta ponerlas tan claras como el lago donde mi papá me enseñó a nadar, y limpia y les da brillo a los pisos hasta que quedan tan lisos que podrías deslizarte por ellos si te quitaras los zapatos.

¿Qué ha cambiado? ¿Cuál es el efecto del cambio?

(A) Todo está silencioso cuando mi mamá entra en el alto edificio de oficinas de vidrio donde ella friega los azulejos de los baños hasta que brillan como la luna limpia las ventanas altas de cristal hasta ponerlas tan claras como el lago donde mi papá me enseñó a nadar, y limpia y les da brillo a los pisos hasta que quedan tan lisos que podrías deslizarte por ellos si te quitaras los zapatos.

(B) Todo estaba silencioso cuando mi mamá entra en el alto edificio de oficinas de vidrio donde ella friega los azulejos de los baños hasta que brillan como la luna, limpia las ventanas altas de cristal hasta ponerlas tan claras como el lago donde mi papá me enseñó a nadar, y limpia y les da brillo a los pisos hasta que quedan tan lisos que podrías deslizarte por ellos si te quitaras los zapatos.

(C) Todo está silencioso cuando mi mamá entra en el alto edificio de oficinas de vidrio donde ella friega los azulejos de los baños, limpia las ventanas altas de cristal hasta ponerlas claras y limpia y les da brillo a los pisos hasta que quedan lisos.

15

Why Do Writers Use Complex Sentences?

¿Por qué los escritores usan las oraciones complejas?

Complex sentences give writers and readers a way to gather ideas together without the separation of a period. In technical terms, complex sentences contain an independent clause and one or more dependent or subordinate clauses, which can be placed anywhere in the sentence—as an opener, interrupter, or closer.

In the end, the most important thing isn't whether we quibble over the definition of *clauses* or *phrases* as much as we understand that some sentence parts can't stand on their own and will need to be connected through meaning to other ideas.

Lesson Sets:

15.1 Las oraciones complejas que comienzan con *cuando*

15.2 Las oraciones complejas con la frase subordinada al final

15.3 Las oraciones complejas con *porque* en el medio de la oración

Correlating English lessons for this chapter can be found in *Patterns of Power*, Chapters 17 and 20.

15.1 Las oraciones complejas que comienzan con *cuando*

Estándar Usar conjunciones subordinantes.

Usar oraciones complejas.

Usar una coma para separar una frase introductoria en una oración.

Frase de enfoque Cuando empiezo una oración con *cuando*, probablemente voy a necesitar usar una coma.

Invitación a notar Cuando escribí Colato, vi a mis abuelos René y Amelia cantando conmigo. Cuando escribí Laínez, vi a mis abuelos Ángela y Julio bailando conmigo.
—René Colato Laínez, *René tiene dos apellidos*

Power Note *If students don't notice the introductory phrase using* cuando, *rewrite the dependent clause on the board as if it is a sentence.*

> *Escribí Colato.*
> *Cuando escribí Colato.*

Ask "¿Cuál es una oración completa y cuál es un fragmento de oración? Platica con tu compañero o compañera." Discuss with students that when cuando *starts a sentence, it will probably need a comma.*

Invitación a comparar Cuando escribí Colato, vi a mis abuelos René y Amelia cantando conmigo. Cuando escribí Laínez, vi a mis abuelos Ángela y Julio bailando conmigo.

Cuando escribo mi nombre, pienso en mi tía por la cual me nombraron así.

Power Note *As students notice how the sentences are alike and different, continue to repeat the focus phrase:* Cuando empiezo una oración con *cuando*, probablemente voy a necesitar usar una coma.

Invitación a imitar *Imitate Together:* Invite writers to use interactive or shared writing to compose a sentence with you.

> Cuando ayudo a mi mamá en la cocina, siempre me da una probadita.

Imitate Independently: Students use the model to create their own sentences using *cuando* as the first word in a sentence.

Invitación a celebrar Students share their *cuando* sentence aloud, saying the word *coma* a bit louder for emphasis.

Invitación a aplicar In pairs have students compose three sentences about their school day that begin with *cuando*.

Invitación a corregir

¿Qué aprendimos de René Colato Laínez acerca de la escritura?	
Cuando escribí Colato, vi a mis abuelos René y Amelia cantando conmigo. Cuando escribí Laínez, via a mis abuelos Ángela y Julio bailando conmigo.	
¿Qué ha cambiado? ¿Cuál es el efecto del cambio?	
(A) Cuando escribí Colato vi a mis abuelos René y Amelia cantando conmigo. Cuando escribí Laínez vi a mis abuelos Ángela y Julio bailando conmigo.	*Faltan las comas después de las frases introductorias. Usamos las comas para separar la frase con* cuando *de la oración que contiene el sujeto y predicado.*
(B) Cuándo escribí Colato, vi a mis abuelos René y Amelia cantando conmigo. Cuándo escribí Laínez, vi a mis abuelos Ángela y Julio bailando conmigo.	*La palabra* cuándo *con un acento escrito normalmente aparece en las preguntas. En este caso,* cuando *no es parte de una pregunta y no lleva acento escrito.*
(C) Cuando escribí Colato, vi a mi abuelos René y Amelia cantando conmigo. Cuando escribí Laínez, vi a mis abuelo Ángela y Julio bailando conmigo.	*Las frases* mi abuelos *y* mis abuelo *no concuerdan. Los pronombres posesivos tienen que concordar con los sustantivos que describen.*

¿Qué notas?

Cuando escribí Colato, vi a mis abuelos René y Amelia cantando conmigo. Cuando escribí Laínez, vi a mis abuelos Ángela y Julio bailando conmigo.

—René Colato Laínez, *René tiene dos apellidos*

¿En qué se parecen? ¿En qué se diferencian?

Cuando escribí Colato, vi a mis abuelos René y Amelia cantando conmigo. Cuando escribí Laínez, vi a mis abuelos Ángela y Julio bailando conmigo.

Cuando escribo mi nombre, pienso en mi tía por la cual me nombraron así.

Inténtalo

Cuando escribí Colato, vi a mis abuelos René y Amelia cantando conmigo. Cuando escribí Laínez, vi a mis abuelos Ángela y Julio bailando conmigo.

Cuando escribo mi nombre, pienso en mi tía por la cual me nombraron así.

Cuando escribí Colato, vi a mis abuelos René y Amelia cantando conmigo. Cuando escribí Laínez, via a mis abuelos Ángela y Julio bailando conmigo.

¿Qué ha cambiado? ¿Cuál es el efecto del cambio?

(A) Cuando escribí Colato vi a mis abuelos René y Amelia cantando conmigo. Cuando escribí Laínez vi a mis abuelos Ángela y Julio bailando conmigo.

(B) Cuándo escribí Colato, vi a mis abuelos René y Amelia cantando conmigo. Cuándo escribí Laínez, vi a mis abuelos Ángela y Julio bailando conmigo.

(C) Cuando escribí Colato, vi a mi abuelos René y Amelia cantando conmigo. Cuando escribí Laínez, vi a mis abuelo Ángela y Julio bailando conmigo.

15.2 Las oraciones complejas con la frase subordinada al final

Estándar Generar una oración compleja.

Frase de enfoque Cuando la frase subordinada viene al final, probablemente no voy a usar una coma.

Invitación a notar Sentí que mis ojos negros se hacían más negros mientras miraba la hoja de la prueba.
—Jane Medina, "La prueba" de *Me llamo Jorge en ambos lados del río*

Power Note *Talk about the effect of putting a comma before* mientras. *Read the sentence both ways. Ask students which version they prefer. By doing this, you are modeling author's purpose and craft. Emphasize that every choice we make as writers has an effect.*

Invitación a comparar Sentí que mis ojos negros se hacían más negros mientras miraba la hoja de la prueba.

Sentí que las lágrimas me corrían mientras veía la nota más baja que había sacado en toda mi vida.

Power Note *Repeat the focus phrase as needed. As students investigate this pattern in other texts, they may find examples in which an author has used a comma before a subordinating conjunction. Discuss why the author might have crafted their sentence that way.*

Invitación a imitar *Imitate Together:* Use shared writing to express that something happened *mientras* something else happened. Use the subordinating conjunction in the middle of the sentence.

El maestro tocó musica relajante mientras tomamos la prueba.

Imitate Independently: Students choose any subordinating conjunction to connect ideas in the middle of a sentence.

Invitación a celebrar As students read aloud their sentences, sharing them twice, highlight the different subordinating conjunctions they use.

Invitación a aplicar Use *Revisión rápida* (see Lesson 5.2) on a current piece of writing to help students look for places they could use a subordinating conjunction to combine or connect ideas. Remind them that each of the conjunctions has a different meaning and therefore a different effect.

Invitación a corregir

¿Qué aprendimos de Jane Medina acerca de la escritura?	
Sentí que mis ojos negros se hacían más negros mientras miraba la hoja de la prueba.	
¿Qué ha cambiado? ¿Cuál es el efecto del cambio?	
(A) Sentí que mis ojos negros se hacían más negros, mientras miraba la hoja de la prueba.	*Una coma aparece antes de* mientras. *"¿Cuál es el efecto cuando leemos la oración en voz alta?" A veces los autores colocan una coma antes de una conjunción subordinada en medio de una oración. Sin embargo, es más común que no usen una coma.*
(B) Sentí que mis ojos negros se hacían más negros hasta que miraba la hoja de la prueba.	*La conjunción subordinada* hasta *indica que algo cambió al ver la prueba.*
(C) Sentí que mis ojos negros se hacían más negros cuando miraba la hoja de la prueba.	*La conjunción subordinada* cuando *indica que al ver la prueba provocó una reacción en el narrador.*

¿Qué notas?

Sentí que mis ojos negros se hacían más negros mientras miraba la hoja de la prueba.

—Jane Medina, "La prueba" de *Me llamo Jorge en ambos lados del río*

¿En qué se parecen? ¿En qué se diferencian?

Sentí que mis ojos negros se hacían más negros mientras miraba la hoja de la prueba.

Sentí que las lágrimas me corrían mientras veía la nota más baja que había sacado en toda mi vida.

Inténtalo

Sentí que mis ojos negros se hacían más negros mientras miraba la hoja de la prueba.

Sentí que las lágrimas me corrían mientras veía la nota más baja que había sacado en toda mi vida.

Cuando escribí Colato, vi a mis abuelos René y Amelia cantando conmigo. Cuando escribí Laínez, via a mis abuelos Ángela y Julio bailando conmigo.

¿Qué ha cambiado? ¿Cuál es el efecto del cambio?

(A) Sentí que mis ojos negros se hacían más negros, mientras miraba la hoja de la prueba.

(B) Sentí que mis ojos negros se hacían más negros hasta que miraba la hoja de la prueba.

(C) Sentí que mis ojos negros se hacían más negros cuando miraba la hoja de la prueba.

15.3 Las oraciones complejas con *porque* en el medio de la oración

Estándar Generar una oración compleja.

Frase de enfoque Cuando uso una frase con *porque* en el medio de una oración, probablemente no voy a usar una coma.

Invitación a notar Ella escribe sus cuentos y poemas en secreto ahora porque no tiene a nadie a quien leérselos.
—Luis J. Rodríguez, *La llaman América*

Power Note *Ask students, "¿Qué hace la palabra* porque *en esta oración?" Because we find variations of* porque *in Spanish (*porque, por qué, el porqué*), remind students that in the middle of a sentence it will almost always be a single, non-accented word.*

Invitación a comparar Ella escribe sus cuentos y poemas en secreto ahora porque no tiene a nadie a quien leérselos.

Escribo un cuento cada día en mi cuaderno porque a mi hermanito le encanta escucharlos.

Power Note *Help students understand that* porque *gives us the cause for something that happens or happened. This is a nice connection to cause-and-effect discussions in reading as well.*

Invitación a imitar *Imitate Together:* Invite writers to compose a sentence with you using *porque*.

> El maestro se puso contento porque todos los estudiantes estaban escribiendo poemas y cuentos cada día.

Imitate Independently: Students use the model to write a sentence using *porque*.

Invitación a celebrar Students read aloud their sentences. When students finish reading, we ask, "¿Qué pasó primero? ¿Cómo lo sabemos?"

Invitación a aplicar In other subjects areas across the day, ask students to defend their thinking by incorporating *porque* into their responses.

Invitación a corregir

¿Qué aprendimos de Jane Medina acerca de la escritura?	
Ella escribe sus cuentos y poemas en secreto ahora porque no tiene a nadie a quien leérselos.	
¿Qué ha cambiado? ¿Cuál es el efecto del cambio?	
(A) Ella escribe sus cuentos y poemas en secreto ahora. Porque no tiene a nadie a quien leérselos.	*La segunda frase es un fragmento de oración. Es una frase que no puede servir como una oración sola.*
(B) Ella escribe sus cuentos y poemas en secreto ahora y no tiene a nadie a quien leérselos.	*La conjunción* y *indica que estos dos sucesos pasan al mismo tiempo. Sin embargo,* y *no demuestra que un suceso causa el otro.*
(C) Porque no tiene a nadie a quien leérselos, ella escribe sus cuentos y poemas en secreto ahora.	*Cambiar el orden de las palabras no afecta el mensaje, pero suena diferente. El autor tiene que decidir cuál fluye mejor.*

¿Qué notas?

Ella escribe sus cuentos y poemas en secreto ahora porque no tiene a nadie a quien leérselos.
—Luis J. Rodríguez, *La llaman América*

¿En qué se parecen? ¿En qué se diferencian?

Ella escribe sus cuentos y poemas en secreto ahora porque no tiene a nadie a quien leérselos.

Escribo un cuento cada día en mi cuaderno porque a mi hermanito le encanta escucharlos.

Inténtalo

Ella escribe sus cuentos y poemas en secreto ahora porque no tiene a nadie a quien leérselos.

Escribo un cuento cada día en mi cuaderno porque a mi hermanito le encanta escucharlos.

Ella escribe sus cuentos y poemas en secreto ahora porque no tiene a nadie a quien leérselos.

¿Qué ha cambiado? ¿Cuál es el efecto del cambio?

(A) Ella escribe sus cuentos y poemas en secreto ahora. Porque no tiene a nadie a quien leérselos.

(B) Ella escribe sus cuentos y poemas en secreto ahora y no tiene a nadie a quien leérselos.

(C) Porque no tiene a nadie a quien leérselos, ella escribe sus cuentos y poemas en secreto ahora.

Acknowledgments

Well, Mr. Anderson, that was one long homework assignment. I hope it fulfills the requirements even if I did turn it in late. Thank you for believing in me then and believing in me all these years later. You listened to me when I was nine and you've listened to me now. You turned an idea into reality. I am forever grateful for the opportunity you have given me to expand on your work. Whitney, you have been my biggest cheerleader behind the scenes. Thanks for propelling me forward even when it was difficult. And a special thanks to some educators and students from Lamar Consolidated ISD who tried out Spanish lessons and shared their work with me: Dianna Bishop, Rosemary Martinez, Yadira Salinas and her students from Travis Elementary School.

To my long-time mentor, Barbara Sassen, you taught me how to teach and stood by me for a decade. Dr. Angie Zapata and Nancy Valdez-Gainer taught me the importance of literature choices in the bilingual classroom. Dr. Doris Villarreal pushed me to reflect on my teaching practice and create space for students to find their power in both languages.

Special thanks to the team at LCpl Nicholas S. Perez Elementary in Austin, Texas. To my principal, Kara Mitchell-Santibañez, who pushes us to be our best for the kids we teach everyday. Beatríz Romero, Michelle González, and Dulce Gómez, thank you for teaching with me and letting me work with your kids to try out lessons (even on Saturdays). I love working alongside the fourth-grade team. Carmela Valdez, thank you for taking a stack of lessons and running with them. Your dedication to authentic writing experiences for our youngest writers inspires me. To my student-teacher-turned-colleague, Kari Johnston, thank you for the hours of working side-by-side, searching for mentor sentences, and listening to me read and reread my writing. Your friendship is invaluable.

To the Stenhouse team, I so appreciate the blind faith you put in me. Bill Varner kept me writing and revising until we got it right. Terry Thompson jumped in and helped me out so much just when I thought I couldn't get it all done. Lynne Costa put it all together in such a beautiful way. A huge thanks to Lesa, Dan, Faye, Jay, and the copyediting team who worked to move this project along quickly.

Most of all, thank you, Jorge, and my sweet boys, Silas and Emil, who had to endure long nights of searching for sentences and writing lessons. You all fill my heart and keep me going. Los amo con todo mi corazón.

Appendix A

Patterns of Power en español Planning Process

Concept: ______________________________

Tema

Standard Estándar	
Author's Purpose/Craft El propósito/estilo del autor	
Focus Phrase Frase de enfoque	
Mentor Sentence/Invitation to Notice Invitación a notar	
Invitation to Compare and Contrast Invitación a comparar	
Invitation to Imitate Invitación a imitar	
Invitation to Celebrate Invitación a celebrar	
Invitation to Apply Invitación a aplicar	
Invitation to Edit Invitación a corregir	Original Mentor Sentence: *¿Qué ha cambiado? ¿Cuál es el efecto del cambio?*
Version 1 Versión 1	
Version 2 Versión 2	
Version 3 Versión 3	

Appendix B

Spanish Lesson Correlation Chart to English Lessons in *Patterns of Power*

Patterns of Power en español **Lesson Number**	**Topic in Spanish**	**Topic in English**	**English Lesson in *Patterns of Power***
2.1	Las letras mayúsculas en los nombres de las personas	Capital letters in people's names	**4.1**
2.2	Las letras mayúsculas en los títulos	Capital letters in titles	**4.4**
2.3	Las letras mayúsculas en el saludo y en la despedida de una carta	Capital Letters in openings and closings of letters	**4.5**
2.4	Las letras mayúsculas en épocas históricas	Capital Letters in historical periods	**4.6**
3.1	Los sustantivos	Nouns	**5.1**
3.2	Cuándo se usa la letra mayúscula y cuándo no	When we capitalize and when we don't	**5.2**
3.3	Los nombres propios de personas y lugares	Proper nouns of people and places	**5.3**
3.4	El plural de los sustantivos	Plural nouns	**5.4**
3.5	Los sustantivos colectivos	Collective nouns	**5.6**
3.6	La acentuación en los sustantivos	Accents in nouns	**None**
4.1	Los verbos demuestran acción	Verbs show action	**6.1**
4.2	El verbo ser	The verb "to be"	**6.2**
4.3	El verbo ser (tiempo futuro)	The verb "to be" future tense	**6.2**
4.4	Los tiempos de los verbos	Verb tenses	**6.3**
4.5	Los verbos irregulares	Irregular Verbs	**6.4**
4.6	Los acentos ortográficos en los verbos pretéritos	Accents in past tense verbs	**None**
5.1	Mi voz y la puntuación	My voice and end punctuation	**8.1**
5.2	Los signos de interrogación	Question marks	**8.2**
5.3	Los signos de admiración	Exclamation points	**8.2**
5.4	Termino mis oraciones: Punto y seguido	I finish my sentences with periods	**8.3**

(continues)

6.1	Los pronombres personales	Personal pronouns	**10.1**
6.2	Los pronombres de segunda persona	Second person pronouns	**10.1**
6.3	Los pronombres posesivos	Possessive pronouns	**10.2**
6.4	Los pronombres reflexivos con verbos	Reflexive pronouns with verbs	**None**
6.5	Los pronombres indefinidos	Indefinite pronouns	**10.3**
7.1	Los sustantivos y verbos como amigos	Nouns and verbs are friends	**11.1**
7.2	Concordancia entre sustantivos y verbos	Subject-verb agreement	**11.2**
7.3	Los sujetos tácitos	Implicit subjects	**None**
7.4	Buscar los verbos que concuerdan en cantidad y persona	Finding verbs that agree in person and number	**11.3**
8.1	Diálogo	Dialogue	**12.2**
8.2	Los paréntesis	Parentheses	**12.4**
9.1	Los adjetivos contestan preguntas	Adjectives answer questions	**13.1**
9.2	Los adjetivos después de los sustantivos	Adjectives after nouns	**13.2**
9.3	Los adjetivos comparativos	Comparative adjectives	**14.1**
9.4	Los adjetivos superlativos	Superlative adjectives	**14.2**
10.1	Los adverbios que demuestran cómo	Adverbs that show how	**15.2**
10.2	Los adverbios que demuestran frecuencia	Adverbs that show how often	**15.3**
10.3	Los adverbios que demuestran dónde	Adverbs that show *where*	**15.4**
11.1	Las preposiciones de *dónde*	Prepositions showing *where*	**16.1**
11.2	Las preposiciones de *cuándo*	Prepositions showing *when*	**16.2**
11.3	Las contracciones *del* y *al*	The contractions *del* and *al*	**9.3**
12.1	La conjunción *y*	The conjunction *and*	**17.1**
12.2	Uso de *o* para mostrar alternativas	Using *or* to show options	**17.5**
12.3	Ni . . . ni	Neither . . . nor	**17.6**
13.1	Combinar oraciones con *y*	Combining sentences with *and*	**18.1**
13.2	Combinar oraciones con *y* o *pero*	Combining sentences with *and* and *but*	**18.2/18.3**
13.3	Combinar oraciones con *sino que*	Combining sentences with *sino que* (no translation other than but)	**18.4**
14.1	La coma serial para separar una lista de verbos	Serial comma to separate verbs in a list	**19.1**
14.2	La coma serial para separar una lista de sustantivos	Serial comma to separate nouns in a list	**19.2**
14.3	La coma serial para separar oraciones compuestas	Serial comma to separate compound sentences	**19.3**
15.1	Las oraciones complejas con *cuando*	Complex sentences starting with *when*	**20.2**
15.2	Las oraciones complejas con la frase subordinada al final	Complex sentences with the subordinate phrase at the end	**20.5**
15.3	Las oraciones complejas con *porque* en el medio	Complex sentences with *because* in the middle	**17.4**

Professional Bibliography

Anderson, Jeff, and Whitney La Rocca. 2017. *Patterns of Power: Inviting Young Writers into the Conventions of Language*, Grades 1–5. Portsmouth, NH: Stenhouse.

Anderson, Jeff. 2007. *Everyday Editing: Inviting Students to Develop Skill and Craft in Writer's Workshop*. Portland, ME: Stenhouse.

Freeman, Yvonne, and David Freeman. 2004. "Connecting Students to Culturally Relevant Texts" *Talking Points* 15 (2): April/May.

Graham, Steve, and Delores Perin. 2007. *Writing Next: Effective Strategies to Improve Writing of Adolescents in Middle and High School—A Report to Carnegie Corporation of New York*. Washington DC: Alliance for Education.

Sims Bishop, R. 1990. "Mirrors, Windows, and Sliding Glass Doors" *Perspectives: Choosing and Using Books for the Classroom* 6 (3): Summer.

Texas Education Agency. 2017. *Texas Essential Knowledge and Skills for Spanish Language Arts and Reading and English as a Second Language* 19 (Ch 128). Austin, TX.: Texas Education Agency.

Thompson, Terry. 2015. *The Construction Zone: Building Scaffolds for Readers and Writers*. Portland, ME: Stenhouse.

Children's Literature Bibliography

Ada, Alma Flor, et al. 2016. *Caminos de José Martí, Frida Kahlo, César Chávez*. Santillana.

Ada, Alma Flor, and F. Isabel Campoy. 2000. *Caballete*. Alfaguara/Santillana.

Ada, Alma Flor, and Gabriel M. Zubizarreta. 2013. *Nacer bailando*. Atheneum Books for Young Readers.

Ada, Alma Flor, and María Jesús Álvarez. 2016. "Bilingüe." *Todo Es Canción: Antología Poética*. Loqueleo.

Aguasaco, Carlos. 2013. "Nueva en Nueva York." *Cool Salsa: Bilingual Poems on Growing Up Latino in the United States*, Paw Prints.

Alba, Juanita, and Peña Amado Maurilio. 2003. *Calor: A Story of Warmth for All Ages*. Lectorum.

Alko, Selina, et al. 2015. *El caso de los Loving: La lucha por el matrimonio interracial*. Scholastic Inc.

Argueta, Jorge. 2016. *La fiesta de las tortillas = The Fiesta of the Tortillas*. Loqueleo.

Argueta, Jorge. 2016. *Somos como las nubes = We Are like the Clouds*. House of Anansi Press.

Argueta, Jorge, and Carl Angel. 2003. *Xochitl and the Flowers = Xochitl, La niña de las flores*. Children's Book.

Argueta, Jorge, and Lucia Angela Perez. "Las Piedras." *Talking with Mother Earth = Hablando con madre tierra: Poems/Poemas*. Groundwood Books/House of Anansi Press, 2006.

Argueta, Jorge, et al. 2017. *Agua, agüita*. Piñata Books, an Imprint of Arte Público Press.

Bertrand, Diane Gonzales, and Gabriela Baeza Ventura. 2006. *The Ruiz Street Kids = Los muchachos de la calle Ruiz*. Piñata Books.

Bertrand, Diane Gonzales, and Hernández Karina. 2004. *Upside down and Backwards = De cabeza y al revés*. Piñata Books.

Brown, Monica, et al. 2013. *Marisol McDonald and the Clash Bash = Marisol McDonald y la fiesta sin igual*. Children's Book Press, an Imprint of Lee & Low Books Inc.

Brown, Monica, et al. 2010. *Side by Side: The Story of Dolores Huerta and Cesar Chavez = Lado a lado: La historia De Dolores Huerta y César Chávez*. Rayo.

Buitrago, Jairo, and Rafael Yockteng. 2016. *Two White Rabbits*. Groundwood Books.

Carlson, Lori M., and Emily Lisker. 1998. "Me gusta montar mi bicicleta." *Sol a Sol: Bilingual Poems*. Henry Holt and Co.

Cervantes, Angela, and Domínguez Jorge Ignacio. 2018. *Frida, el misterio del anillo del pavo real y yo*. Scholastic Inc.

Cohn, Diana, and Francisco Delgado. 2013. *Sí, ¡Se Puede! = Yes, We Can!: Janitor Strike in L.A.* Zaner-Bloser.

Garza, Carmen Lomas. 1996. *In My Family = En mi familia*. Children's Book Press.

Garza, Xavier, and Gabriela Baeza Ventura. 2010. *Kid Cyclone Fights the Devil: And Other Stories = Kid Ciclón se enfrenta a El Diablo: y Otras Historias*. Piñata Books.

Gonzalez, Eric, and Erich Haeger. 2010. *Rosita y Conchita: A Rhyming Storybook in English & Spanish*. Muertoons.

Gonzalez, Maya Christina. 2012. *I Know the River Loves Me = Yo sé que el río me ama*. Children's Book Press.

González Saraí, et al. 2019. *Saraí salva la música*. Scholastic Inc.

Hayes, Joe, and Antonio Castro. 2003. *The Day It Snowed Tortillas = El día que nevaron tortillas: Folktales Told in Spanish and English*. Cinco Puntos.

Herrera, Juan Felipe., and Elizabeth Gómez. 2006. *The Upside Down Boy = El niño de cabeza*. Children's Book Press.

Lainez, René Colato. 2009. *René Has Two Last Names = René tiene dos apellidos*. Piñata Books.

Laínez, René Colato, and Fabricio Vanden Broeck. 2019. *My Shoes and I: Crossing Three Borders*. Piñata Books, an Imprint of Arte Publico Press.

Laínez, René Colato, and Joe Cepeda. 2014. *From North to South = Del Norte al Sur*. Children's Book Press.

Martinez-Neal, Juana. 2018. *Alma and How She Got Her Name = Alma y cómo obtuvo su nombre*. Candlewick Press.

Mateo José Manuel, et al. 2014. *Migrant = Migrar*. Abrams Books for Young Readers.

Medina, Jane, and Fabricio Vanden Broeck. 1999. *My Name Is Jorge on Both Sides of the River = Me llamo Jorge en ambos lados del río*. Wordsong/Boyds Mills Press.

Mills, Deborah, Alfredo Alva, and Claudia Navarro. 2018. *La Frontera: El Viaje Con Papá = My Journey with Papa*. Barefoot Books.

Mora, Pat, et al. 1997. *Tomás y la señora de la biblioteca*. Dragonfly Books.

Mora, Pat, and Rafael López. 2009. "Chocolate." *Yum! Mmmm! ¡Qué rico!: Brotes de las Américas*. Lee & Low Books.

Morales, Yuyi. 2016. *Little Night = Nochecita*. Square Fish/Roaring Brook Press.

Morales, Yuyi. Translated by Teresa Mlawer. 2018. *Soñadores*. Neal Porter Books.

Pérez, Amada Irma., and Maya Christina Gonzalez. 2009. *My Diary from Here to There = Mi diario de aquí hasta allá*. Lee & Low Books, Inc.

Nye, Naomi Shihab. "Piñata." 1998. *The Tree Is Older than You Are: A Bilingual Gathering of Poems & Stories from Mexico with Paintings by Mexican Artists*. Aladdin Paperbacks.

Ramos, Jorge, and Akemi Gutierrez. 2008. *I'm Just like My Mom: Me parezco tanto a mi mamá*. Rayo.

Reynolds, Peter H. 2018. *The Word Collector = El coleccionista de palabras*. Orchard Books, an Imprint of Scholastic Inc.

Rivera-Ashford, Roni Capin, and Antonio Castro. *My Tata's Remedies = Los remedios de mi tata*. Cinco Puntos Press, 2015.

Rodriguez, Luis J. 1998. *América Is Her Name = La llaman América*. Curbstone Press.

Saldaña René, and Carolina Villarroel. 2009. *The Case of the Pen Gone Missing = El caso de la pluma perdida*. Piñata Books/Arte Público Press.

Sáenz Benjamin Alire., and Esau Andrade. 2010. *A Perfect Season for Dreaming = Un tiempo perfecto para soñar*. Cinco Puntos Press.

Senties, Raquel Valle. "Soy como soy y qué." 2013. *Cool Salsa: Bilingual Poems on Growing Up Latino in the United States*, Paw Prints.

Soto, Gary, et al. 1993. *¡Qué montón de tamales!* PaperStar.

Tafolla, Carmen, and Magaly Morales. 2014. *What Can You Do with a Paleta? = ¿Qué puedes hacer con una paleta?* Dragonfly.

Telgemeier, Raina. 2017. *Fantasmas*. Paw Prints.

Tonatiuh, Duncan, and Eida de la Vega. 2017. *Querido Primo: Una Carta a Mi Primo*. Scholastic, Inc.

Tonatiuh, Duncan, and Graciela Romero. 2018. *La Princesa y El Guerrero: Historia De Dos Volcanes*. V & R Editoras.

Winter, Jeanette, and Jonah Winter. 1994. *Diego*. Knopf.

Winter, Jeanette, and Susana Tornero. 2013. *Biblioburro: Una historia real de Colombia*. Juventud.

Woodson, Jacqueline, and Rafael López. 2018. *The Day You Begin = El día en que descubres quién eres*. Nancy Paulsen Books.

Yolen, Jane, et al. 1996. *Encuentro*. Harcourt Brace & Co.

Yousafzai, Malala, et al. 2017. *El lápiz mágico de Malala*. Little, Brown and Company.

Zepeda, Gwendolyn, et al. 2009. *Growing up with Tamales = Los tamales de Ana*. Piñata Books.

Index

Page numbers followed by *f* indicate figures.

D

E

F

G

H

I

K

L

Q

R

S

T

U

V

W

X

Y

Z